No Higher Call

A Biblical Treatise on Adoption

by

Bradford Smith

Published by

Olivia Kimbrell Press™

Copyright Notice

No Higher Call: a Biblical Treatise on Adoption

First edition. Copyright © 2015 by Bradford Smith. All rights reserved. No part of this publication may be reproduced or transmitted in any form or by any means — electronic, mechanical, photocopying, or recording — without express written permission of the author. The only exception is brief quotations in printed or broadcasted critical articles and reviews. This book is a work of nonfiction. Specific names and places of individuals and towns may have been changed in order to protect the privacy of those involved or where required by law in the case of minor children.

PUBLISHED BY: Olivia Kimbrell Press™*, P.O. Box 4393, Winchester, KY 40392-4393

The *Olivia Kimbrell Press*™ colophon and open book logo are trademarks of Olivia Kimbrell Press™. **Olivia Kimbrell Press™ is a publisher offering true to life, meaningful fiction from a Christian worldview intended to uplift the heart and engage the mind.*

Some scripture quotations courtesy of the King James Version (KJV) of the Holy Bible. Some scripture quotations taken from the Holman Christian Standard Bible® (HCSB), Copyright© 1999, 2000, 2002, 2003, 2009 by Holman Bible Publishers. Used by permission. All rights reserved. Some scripture quotations courtesy of the New King James Version (NKJV) of the Holy Bible, Copyright© 1979, 1980, 1982 by Thomas-Nelson, Inc. Used by permission. All rights reserved.

Original Cover Art and Graphics by Debi Warford (www.debiwarford.com)

Library Cataloging Data
U.S. Library of Congress Control Number (PCN): 2015939519

Smith, Bradford. (Bradford Smith) 1973-
 No Higher Call; a Biblical Treatise on Adoption/Bradford Smith
  142 p. 20.32cm x 12.7cm (8in x 5in.)
Summary: Gripping, confrontational, in your face - No Higher Call, a biblical treatise on adoption, will drive you to action.

ISBN-13: 978-1-939603-89-0 (Perfect Print on Demand)

1. Fostering 2. Adoption 3. Orphans 4. Fatherless 5. Widows

No Higher Call

A Biblical Treatise on Adoption

by

Bradford Smith

TABLE OF CONTENTS

No Higher Call 1
   Copyright Notice 2
   Table of Contents 4
   Dedication 6
   Acknowledgement 7
Introduction 8
Chapter One — First Call/Last Call 13
   Chapter One Discussion Questions 18
Chapter Two — The Will 20
   Chapter Two Discussion Questions 51
Chapter Three — The Need 53
   Chapter Three Discussion Questions 70
Chapter Four — The Call 72
   Chapter Four Discussion Questions 97
Chapter Five — The Blood 99
   Chapter Five Discussion Questions 110
Chapter Six — The Champion 112
   Chapter Six Discussion Questions 124

Chapter Seven — Tender Healers	126
Final Discussion Questions	134
Personal Note	136
Bibliography	137
Glossary of Terms	138
About the Author	140
Also Available	141
More to Come	142

DEDICATION

DEDICATED to my beautiful wife Ami, the greatest champion of the Orphan I know…

ACKNOWLEDGEMENTS

I am forever indebted to my good friend and mentor, Kevin Schmidt from Military Community Youth Ministries in Hawaii, for first pulling the sword from the stone and then explaining it to the likes of me.

 INTRODUCTION

FOR three weeks now I've been shaking my fist at God. It's difficult to shake your fist at God while simultaneously holding a baby, but it can be done. Of this, I assure you. In anger, in frustration, I've been raging against God. God has called me to a number of things but recently he's placed an unwelcome call upon my life, upon my heart.

God has sent us another baby, a boy, born into unimaginable circumstances and in sovereignty, He has placed him, quite literally, in my arms. He has called me again to *father* and stunningly, it is the absolute last thing I want at this particular point in my life and so I've raged.

God I don't want this!

God I'm too old for this!

God this doesn't have to be my responsibility!

Why can't someone else do this?

This just isn't fair.

My lamentations have thus far fallen upon deaf ears. Days ago I sat and fed Hector and as his solemn and helpless eyes contemplated my weary countenance, I kept hearing the quiet whisper of the Spirit in my heart, "It's not his fault; it's not his fault." Over and over. It would not subside, this drumbeat. *It's not his fault.* As my heart has begun to soften, I've raged against that as well, my softening heart, but I can see that my resistance is steadily fading, futile even. I do not possess the strength to resist this call much longer.

The Orphan, spiritual and otherwise, lies at the heart of Scripture. In this work, I seek to firmly implant in your mind that which Scripture says concerning those who have no family, those who have no home, the Orphan.

The Call is reserved for God's people alone and never before has the world so desperately needed the people of God to *act*. In addressing God's people, I seek to impress upon you, Believer, the full weight of God's Word upon this increasingly deterministic issue.

I'll ask you to consider many different things, many different aspects and ideas throughout the course of this work, but most of all, I'll ask that you examine the condition of your heart. **Where exactly is your heart?**

As the seat of the will, the heart drives our actions. If you are a believer, then God has given you a new heart. *He* has replaced your heart of stone with a heart of flesh and so I'll ask again, where is your heart? Is it calloused? Will you harden your heart to this message, to the Call?

Whatever the condition of your own heart, rest assured that many languish in affliction, desperate for the love and *action* of God's people, those allowing the endless love of the Father to pour forth. O' Believer, I pray in desperation that you'll consider your heart as you consider this call. Will you yield?

I think you'll be astonished at the sheer clarity with which the Bible speaks concerning the Orphan. Cast theological dictums to the curb, they are as unnecessary as the unintelligible language with which some veil their arguments though I have included a glossary of theological terms just in case. But the clarity; it cuts across the grain of our personal comfort, confronting us where it may just possibly hurt the most. In confession, I possess a vested interest, a personal stake.

Yet, I pray that the Holy Spirit would be the Illuminator of the truth contained herein, not that emotion or my vague ramblings might somehow guilt a person into consideration of this most serious issue. Remove the emotion, remove the passion, remove the rhetoric, and I'll argue that what remains is a very astonishing collection of telling facts and clear biblical insight that has no other possibility than to generate that which I have sought to eliminate from consideration – emotion and passion. In fact, that emotion and passion might just compel one does not render the action illegitimate. Quite the contrary.

Reason, and that which most consider reasonable, at least from an earthly perspective, cannot and does not drive or dictate that which is greatest. Our Heavenly Father, as He ordained the Plan from eternity past assured us of this. Reasonability did not drive Stephen to boldly declare, "Brothers and fathers, listen!" (Acts 7:2) as he stood accused before the Sanhedrin, his spilt blood testifying for eternity to the sheer absence of reasonability in his commitment.

Wilberforce, Muller, Judson, the Moravians, all gave very little, if any, consideration to that which most consider reasonable. Reasonability was the furthest thing from the mind of our Lord as He suffered at Golgotha. Indeed, it would seem that an absence of consideration for reason would almost be a prerequisite for that which is the greatest. Yet, so many worship the god of reason – myself included on occasion.

Still, I will appeal to your sense of reason. As I appeal to your heart, your passion, your emotion, I'll appeal to reason…godly reason.

William Carey, the father of modern missions, stood before his fellow pastors urging them to establish a missionary agency so that Christ might be proclaimed to the nations. "Young man, sit down. When God pleases to convert the heathen, he'll do it without consulting you or me," was the less than encouraging response from a prominent elder.[1] This man had stared down godly reason, manifest in Carey's passion, and declared it foolishness, certainly unreasonable.

Carey remained undaunted, later establishing the Baptist Missionary Society and subsequently transforming the missional world, re-introducing a new, but long-forgotten way. He simply would not be denied. Christ drove him and even after seven years in India without a single convert, he persisted, preaching in his *Deathless Sermon*, "Expect great things from God, attempt great things for God."[2]

I'm talking about a marriage, a union between zeal and reason, godly reason. Courage is the natural offspring of such a coupling.[3] The courage to try, the fortitude to endeavor, the strength to undertake: all of these undergird the actions of those compelled in the manner of Carey.

And so, on behalf of the Lord, at the behest of the Orphan, I'll ask you to consider that which many might consider unreasonable. I'll unabashedly seek to stoke the flames of your passion, to fan them into a consuming fire with the very pages of the Bible. I'll pray that you'll be consumed by compassion for the Orphan. I pray that this work will *affect* you but, I understand your hesitation.

I currently battle the Call. I've locked horns with the biblical

---

[1] Diane Severance, "William Carey's Amazing Mission," accessed March 2015,(http://www.christianity.com/church/church-history/timeline/1701-1800/william-careys-amazing-mission-11630319.html).

[2] Ken Curtis, "William Carey's Deathless Sermon," accessed March 2015, (http://www.christianity.com/church/church-history/timeline/1701-1800/william-careys-deathless-sermon-11630318.html). To this day, Carey is revered in parts of India. He is memorialized in numerous places. Schools teach the children about him.

[3] A forthright discussion with a mentor of mine, Kevin Schmidt of Military Community Youth Ministries in Hawaii, yielded the notion that I could not reject godly reason. The disparity between that which most consider reasonable and godly reason must be considered as most of the remainder of this work relies upon an appeal to the godly reason of the reader to invoke compassion and call the believer to action.

Awesome on account of reason, or my perceptions of that which is reasonable. What do you do when God issues an unwelcome call, when you cannot possibly conceive how you would accomplish that to which God is calling you? This isn't the first time I've struggled in such a manner.

Years ago, our family even suspended the Call on behalf of reason, reason as I saw it rather, and only the persistence of my loving spouse and the unbridled faith of my two young daughters, illuminating the necessity on behalf of God of that which I had considered unreasonable, reminded me that…

… there is *No Higher Call*.

> For you did not receive the
> spirit of bondage again to fear,
> but you received the
> Spirit of adoption
> by whom we cry out, "Abba, Father."
>
> Romans 8:15 (NKJV)

Chapter 1

AS a young man, I had it made, or so I thought. I lived the high-life with no concern for anyone but myself. I went wherever I wanted and did whatever I wanted to do. I lived completely immersed in my own existence never having to consider another. I lived completely free to seek the absolute gratification of my own self in any way that I wanted and I was absolutely miserable and lonely. Life rang hollow of meaning, devoid of purpose, empty.

That's when I got my cart before my horse. If I've piqued your interest at all, if I've done even a serviceable job of hooking you in, perhaps you wonder about my actual family situation. "Just how many children do you have?" Interestingly enough, that is a moderately difficult question that I am often asked, but usually don't really know how to answer and not for the reasons you may think.

A friend and I watched the movie *9 ½ Weeks* once. In it, Mickey Rourke played the smooth, rich single guy who has a torrid love affair with a beautiful blonde woman portrayed by Kim Basinger. At the time, he epitomized my notion of cool but it's his closet that I remember the most. The woman finds herself in his apartment by herself and so she does what women tend to do, she looked around a bit. Okay, she snooped. When she opened his closet, there hung a row of identical, perfectly pressed suits. Nothing else. I remember thinking that was the coolest thing I'd ever seen.

I wanted to be Mickey Rourke; I certainly didn't want to be a father. Parenthood just never appealed to me. It scared me actually – the notion of fatherhood and all that came along with it. I had no inkling, no desire, no drive to ever father children, and this condition persisted well into my adult years as I lived much of my early adult life desperately seeking to fashion myself into that which I sought to emulate.

My desires had little to do with my own family. I had a rather normal, middle class upbringing; one brother, blue-collar parents, middle-class suburbia. My father worked hard his entire life and taught my brother and me the value of hard work. He loved us and took good care of us. I just had no desire to be a father myself.

Instead, I idolized my aunt. My mother's sister, my Aunt Esther, served as an Army nurse and traveled the world, literally. She remained single her entire life and always had a cool car, lots of money, and lived, from, what I could tell, a very exciting existence.

I remember visiting her in Germany once. She had so many stories of the amazing people she interacted with and the amazing places she had visited. I wanted to be like her. My brother could be the father, but not me. Who on earth would want to stay at home and wipe a bunch of literal and proverbial snotty noses when the whole world beckoned? Not me. I would be rich, single Uncle Brad! For a while, that is precisely how things went.

I lived this supposed dream for several years. I graduated from college, went to flight school, got stationed in Korea, then Honduras, living the single life, living my dream, traveling the globe. My brother, meanwhile, married a girl who already had two young boys and became an instant father. I still remember blasting into town to visit them playing the role of rich, single Uncle Brad with the cool car and the stories of traveling the world. Well, as rich as an Army guy could be anyway.

I remember one day a number of years ago my father and I ran into Mr. McBride. His son David had been my best friend growing up. As my Dad and I inquired about his sons' well-being, he informed us that one of them, I can't remember which, was doing well as a father, but hadn't gotten married yet. Mr. McBride wryly informed us that "He got his cart before his horse."

At the time of this writing, my wife Ami and I have five children that legally belong to us, three daughters and two sons. We are also the legal guardians, for going on two years, of our little Mexican guy, Juan Miguel. Lord willing, Juan Miguel will become my third son. Our two foster sons, brothers aged 14 and 11, have lived with us for nearly two years as well. Lord willing, they will also become my sons. Baby Hector just arrived, another son. Yes, if you're counting, that's nine children. Ours is a busy household, but it all started when I got my cart before my horse.

As I prepared to write this chapter, my wife sent me a picture from church. I had been out of town for several weeks conducting some Army training in preparation for an impending deployment to Afghanistan. In the picture, Ami smiles from the bathroom mirror with my two little brown guys, DJ and Juan Miguel, hanging off her legs, smiling back up at me. She tells me that whenever Juan Miguel, age 3, sees a helicopter flying overhead, he points at it and squeals, "Daddy!" Words could never capture my love for those two little brown guys.

I met Ami at the club of all places. Looking back, I can't quite believe it happened the way it did, but I was deeply into my dream. I had become Mickey Rourke. As a young, single flight school student, a lieutenant, I lived the high life. I even wore my slightly out of regulations hair slicked back with gel, just as cool as I could be. That's when I saw her. I was taken, instantly. Her long brown hair framed her beautiful, delicate face. She had the most intense, deep blue eyes I'd ever seen. I asked her to dance. Surprisingly, she said yes. So began our own month's long torrid love affair until it all came crashing to a halt.

Ami informed me that she was pregnant and the Army informed me that I was heading to Korea. I'll spare you the sordid details of the next few years of my life, but let's just say that it took me awhile to get things sorted out. Why do I relay such details to you now? I seek to impress upon you a sense of transparency in the matter we are about to discuss, and to dispel any notion that I may possess any sense of superiority related to the matter this work will examine.

The fact is, I couldn't have done things any worse. I don't think there were very many mistakes I didn't make. I know for certain I could not have strayed further from how God would have had me do things. Yet, in His mercy, in His infinite wisdom, He sorted things out for me, on my behalf. The more I ran from Him – the more I tried to sort things out on my own – the worse things became.

Today, Ami and I are happily married for going on 14 years and both of us will tell you, "but by the grace of our Lord and Savior Christ Jesus." Our marriage likely would not have endured if not for God imposing His will upon our lives. I certainly would not be the father He has molded me into today, the father I still seek to become, or that I have yet to become.

I feel I must confide in you a bit. I've struggled greatly with the heart of this message, reconciling it with consideration for you the reader. Don't be misled, I pray fervently that some of you, all of you perhaps, may feel led to at least consider adoption or fostering, to consider caring for an orphan. I pray that some of you may feel compelled to support fostering and adoption; there are innumerable ways.

As our congregation discussed how to mobilize the church on this issue a young lady offered, "You just have to keep getting in people's faces about it." Though the phrasing may be slightly rough, the idea contains validity. Through my attempts at transparency, I've sought to convey the essence of the struggle. As life hangs in the balance, God rarely mitigates demands for the sake of expediency or comfort. The Call simply is.

As I can, I've sought to faithfully convey what the Bible says concerning the Call. Certainly my emotional investment resonates. How can it not? Each of you, O Believer, exists at a different place in your walk with the Lord. Similarly, my union of zeal and godly reason as it pertains to the Orphan has not always pervaded; it has evolved. I've struggled much. I pray you'll see this.

I always wanted to be Mickey Rourke. God wanted me to be Abraham, or Gideon maybe. **My sons – present and future – needed me to be a father.** The intersection of these – God, me, my sons – wove together an existence, a living embodiment of the very heart of our Creator, epitomized by the plight of the Orphan and the ordained institution of adoption. I can think of *No Higher Call.*

QUESTIONS

1. Review Joel 2:25.

    a. What is the context of this verse?

    b. Verse 18 seems to indicate a change in tone from the previous sections. Why is this? How do you reconcile this apparent change in God's stance with the immutability of God?

    c. What does Joel mean when addressing "the years the locust ate"?

    d. What does it mean that he will restore these years or repay them?

2. What are common things that people regret later in life? Why do they miss these things the first time?

3. What are some things that you perhaps regret? Do you have years that the locust has eaten?

4. Has God restored or repaid these years to you?

5. Why does God allow the locust to "eat" years sometimes?

> *Is* this not the fast that I have chosen:
> To loose the bonds of wickedness,
> To undo the heavy burdens,
> To let the oppressed go free,
> And that you break every yoke?
>
> *Is it* not to share your bread with the hungry,
> And that you bring to your house the poor who are cast out;
> When you see the naked, that you cover him,
> And not hide yourself from your own flesh?
>
> Isaiah 58:6-7 (NKJV)

Chapter 2

GOD has spoken clearly concerning the Orphan. Rest assured, God has a will for your life, a plan, written in eternity past, and His will must be accomplished, it shall certainly be accomplished. Believer, the pages of the Bible, God's inerrant and eternal living Word, come alive, illuminating what He would have you do. As I intend to address this very specific aspect of the will of God concerning you, the Believer, and the Orphan, I must first address some generalities. Before I can present the specified will of God concerning the Orphan, I must first address the totality of His will.

Of Those Who Seek

WHAT *is the Lord's will for my life,* an unnerving and irritating query if there ever was one? As a pastor, Christians often ask me these questions: *What does God want me to do? Where does He want me to go? Does He want me to do this or does He want me to do that?* Of those who truly seek God's will, I have noticed essentially three distinct types of people.

First are those who literally seek the Lord's will for each and every aspect of their lives and, almost annoyingly to me, appear quite successful at discerning just what it is God wants them to do at any given moment. I have several friends that fit rather smugly into this category. They rarely appear to doubt. They truly appear as if, and constantly indicate, they are operating exactly in the center of God's will in every aspect of their existence; from where they live, to what car they drive, to what it is that they actually *do*.

These particularly annoying people always seem to be seeking and discerning, and perhaps an aspect of dependency defines the relationship between discernment and seeking. It would certainly seem to be very difficult to discern that which you do not seek, and logic, human logic anyway, would certainly dictate that the more ravenously you seek something, the more likely that you will find it.

Second are those professing believers who do not seek the will of God or maybe seek it sporadically, occasionally. I'll seek it for that deemed important, when it really matters, but for the routine, day-to-day decisions and operations, instead of considering God I'll rely upon my own intuition and judgment. After all, is it not the Lord that equips us with this intuition and judgment in the first place? A sense of complacency seems to dominate these particularly blissful folks.

Lastly are those who actively seek the will of God for their lives but have great difficulty, a category which I believe encompasses most believers at some point in their lives. The will of God seems to evade them and they become greatly frustrated, angry even. They cannot understand why God doesn't just speak more clearly. Where is the voice from the proverbial burning bush? Demoralized, they point to those in the Bible who hear the voice of God very clearly and say, "See!", or they point to one of those mentioned above, one of those odious individuals who are smugly confident in their will-centeredness, and they become greatly discouraged.

"Why doesn't God speak to me?"

"Why can't I hear his voice?"

"What am I doing wrong?"

Some even misunderstand Scripture, drawing misleading conclusions about their actual relationship with the Lord as a function of their seeming inability to hear the voice of the Lord clearly. The words of the Lord, Jesus:

My sheep hear My voice, I know them, and they follow Me.
John 10:27

"If the sheep, the believers, hear Jesus' voice, but I don't hear His voice, then perhaps I am not one of the sheep," goes the logic leading to a number of misleading conclusions even, "am I really saved?"

Am I really saved?!

I do not intend to exegetically address the erroneous nature of this type of poisonous thinking. Never mind the fact that a non-believer would surely not consider or seriously seek to consider the will of God and factor it into their life. Jesus spoke, in this passage, concerning the issue of salvation and if you responded in faith to the call of God at some point in your life, then you have heard God's voice at least once. Maybe it just happened – hallelujah! – or maybe it happened some time ago. Either way, you are not a believer if you have not heard the voice of the Lord and responded.

Yet, many become intensely frustrated at their seeming inability to discern what God wants them to do. They know that they ought to do *something*. They hear preachers preach about it, hopefully. They see others doing things. Perhaps the Holy Spirit whispers quietly in their ear, "get busy." They see the needs, the lost, and they know, they *know*, that they should be doing something.

I've noticed an interesting condition develop, paralysis. I've seen Christians paralyzed by indecision and fear. *I know I should do something, but I don't know what and I don't want to do the wrong thing. What if I do the wrong thing and I anger God?*

I wonder if perhaps the fathers struggled so. Did Paul wrangle himself to death trying to discern if he should first go to Derbe or Lystra? Did he anguish over the decision to choose Timothy? Did Peter hesitate before going to Caesarea to visit Cornelius? Was he wracked with doubt?

Certainly the Apostles and the fathers were fallible men, and certainly they had doubts and fears just like the rest of us. The Bible does not contain an exhaustive reference to *everything* that has ever happened. Were things just different then?

Macedonia

WHY does it seem as if so many professing believers struggle today? Perhaps they think about things *too* much. Perhaps they try *too* hard. Maybe things are actually much simpler than they would dare think. First, I must ask, do they seek the Father's will from the one place guaranteed to speak clearly as the living, breathing, inerrant Word of God, the Bible? Follow with me,

> *Long ago God spoke to the fathers by the prophets at different times and in different ways. In these last days, He has spoken to us by His Son...*

Hebrews 1:1,2a

The will of God is knowable. Though the Father Himself is shrouded in mystery and certainly many aspects of His will are yet to be revealed, He has revealed Himself to us in the person of the Son and if He speaks to us, He speaks through the Son and the one caveat to comprehension is that *we must know the Son.*

As such, Jesus, the Son of God, God incarnate, speaks loud and clear from the revealed Word of God, the Bible. Scripture affirms that He has indeed spoken to us. Unfortunately, sometimes He says things we don't exactly desire to hear.

All Scripture is inspired by God and is profitable for teaching, for rebuking, for correcting, for training in righteousness, so that the man of God may be complete, equipped for every good work.

2 Timothy 3:16,17

Paul affirms the inspiration and sufficiency of Scripture. The Bible provides all that we need, equipping the believer, not just for some good works, but for *every* good work. We have no need for any other motivation or foundation. The revealed Word of God as recorded in the Bible provides believers with all that they would ever need. We must first and always seek the voice of the Lord concerning His will from the pages of Scripture.

The will of God permeates every single page of the Bible. The Bible clearly addresses the revealed will of God and in many cases, the revealed will of God for believers in a strikingly specific fashion. We must, however, start general and work toward a more specific application.

To affirm, first and foremost, we must seek the will of God. As a believer, the Holy Spirit has overcome my most basic and primal will, to rebel against God, and He has brought me into communion with the Father through the Son. I have a new nature, a new heart, a will that no longer serves itself. My nature has become bent toward God. I still struggle with the old ways, but they must wane.

> *There is a way that seems right to a man, but its end is the way to death.*
>
> Proverbs 14:12

Man's way, my will, my original nature, provides nothing but a pathway to destruction. God's ways, God's will, provides a worthy pursuit… the only pursuit, in fact, worth reckoning.

Our Lord Himself acknowledged this very notion.

> *I can do nothing on My own. I judge only as I hear, and My judgment is righteous, because I do not seek My own will, but the will of Him who sent Me.*
>
> John 5:30
>
> *For I have come down from heaven, not to do My will, but the will of Him who sent Me.*
>
> John 6:38

The Son acknowledges the primacy, the *onlyness*, of the Father's will. The Son acknowledges His helplessness apart from the Father. God incarnate has sought the will of the Father, and as imitators of Christ, how can we do less? It is right that we seek the will of the Father. Anything other than that – my own will – leads only to futility, the way of death. The striking aspect of the dichotomy leads to a fundamental conclusion. No middle ground exists. I either serve God or I serve myself.

It is right that we seek the will of God in *all* things. We ought to strive to align everything in our lives with Christ.

And whatever you do, in word or in deed, do everything in the name of the Lord Jesus,

Colossians 3:17a

Paul exhorts the Colossians, and by application, believers, to do everything in the name of the Lord. We should work in the name of the Lord. We should think in the name of the Lord. Our relationships ought to reflect Christ. Our recreation ought to reflect Christ. No caveats exist to soften the demand. Paul provides no exceptions to lessen the impact. A few sentences later, he says,

Whatever you do, do it enthusiastically [lit. do it from the soul], as something done for the Lord and not for men,

Colossians 3:23

Do all things for God and do them with enthusiasm, literally from the soul. Passion, commitment, and zeal should undergird all that we do. When we do things on behalf of the Creator, the Father, as ambassadors for Christ, how can we help but not act with passion, from the soul, as Paul speaks.

Realistically, it is not as if the created could thwart the will of the Creator. As it were, God has a purpose and a plan, a will for all men, and Scripture tells us,

The LORD will fulfill His purpose for me,

Psalm 138:8

His will shall be done; what He has ordained from eternity past will be accomplished. The Bible affirms this very notion as it affirms the notion of the perseverance of His will.

Many plans are in a man's heart, but the LORD's decree will prevail.

Proverbs 19:21

O believer, draw a measure of comfort from this notion. Quit tearing yourself apart seeking that which already happens, that which the Lord has already decided and ordained. The LORD's will is unthwartable. You could no more impede the will of the Father than a grain of sand could divert a rushing river, or a speck of dust could shield you from the Sun. You may not recognize the will of the Father this side of glory, but the will of God is inevitable. Rest well and know that He is God.

Or do you seek the will of God for a reason other than pure obedience and joy in serving Him, that His will may be accomplished? If your primary concern is God and that His will be accomplished, would not the fact that His will shall certainly be accomplished no matter what you do or don't do ease this self-induced pressure to discern with complete accuracy that which God speaks.

Perhaps, brothers and sisters, you possess another motive. Do your feelings generate this angst? Listen to the subject of these common statements:

I want to know the will of God.

I want to serve God.

I want to be useful in His sight.

Contrast that with the simple, obedient proclamation of the Lord, our God,

"Thy will be done."

Do you see the subtle yet telling shift in focus from self to

God?

Do you truly seek to worship and serve God with the purest of notions? It is not as if the things you are doing or are not doing were not ordained by God in eternity past. Do you really think that God would punish you if you got it "wrong"? O Believer, a spirit certainly generates these ideas, but not the Spirit. Look to the Scriptures.

They [Paul and Timothy] went through the region of Phrygia and Galatia, and were prevented by the Holy Spirit from speaking the message in the province of Asia.

Acts 16:6

This is the Apostle Paul and Timothy, seeking to serve God, to speak the Message, but God prevented them from speaking it in Asia. Certainly God desired that someone would speak the message in Asia, certainly a good and godly thing. God just didn't desire that Paul and Timothy speak the message in Asia at that particular time.

Did the Lord smite him for his disobedience? Did the Lord punish him for getting it "wrong"? No. He merely diverted him on his path.

The Lord intended for him to evangelize Macedonia and so that is where He directed him. The Lord *willed* that Paul and Timothy would evangelize Macedonia and even though they did not recognize it immediately, this is exactly what occurred.

It is right that we seek the will of God. Lay aside your assault upon the fortress walls of forbidden Asia and heed God's gentle push toward Macedonia. Many there await your efforts.

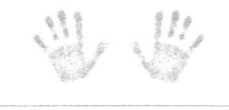

Fundamentals

ONCE we acknowledge the inevitability and overpowering totality of the will of God, we must recognize that most basic command for Christians, known as the Great Commission. God dispatches His people to deliver His good news, the good news of the Gospel of Christ Jesus. Following the Resurrection, Jesus says to the believers,

> *All authority has been given to Me in heaven and on earth. Go, therefore, and make disciples of all nations baptizing them in the name of the Father and of the Son and of the Holy Spirit, teaching them to observe everything I have commanded you.*

Matthew 28: 18b-20a

The only imperative herein is the command, make disciples. Jesus clearly commands believers to make disciples, modified by the participles of going, baptizing, and teaching. As we make disciples, we are to go, to baptize and to teach. God's primary command for all believers resonates in its simplicity, though many have written volumes concerning the subject of making disciples, how to make disciples, what it means to make disciples.

Prior to the Ascension, while the Lord fellowshipped with the believers in Jerusalem He said,

> *But you will receive power when the Holy Spirit has come upon you, and you will be My witnesses in Jerusalem, in all Judea and Samaria, and to the ends of the earth.*

Acts 1:8

Here, Jesus issues a passive command, nothing a believer could affect. "Be empowered by the Holy Spirit," He commands.

The Holy Spirit will empower believers. We have no choice and, furthermore, we *will* be witnesses, in many different places, Jerusalem, Judea, Samaria, the ends of the earth. God empowers believers with the Holy Spirit for a very specific reason. God empowers believers to witness, to testify.

Believers, per Jesus, will attest to what they have seen per 1 John 1:1-3 to people everywhere, to every nation, to the Samaritans, to the ends of the earth. Again, scholars have written countless volumes concerning the logical outflow of this particular command of Christ and specific applications, but fundamentally, God commands believers to witness, to testify to what they have seen, what they have heard, what they have experienced.

With this, one can say quite clearly that God wills that you make disciples and act as a witness. These two commands must undergird every aspect of all that believers do. They must serve as screening criteria, a lamp-stand to illuminate the underlying motives of our actions, and so I ask of you who struggle,

Do you make disciples?

Do you go, baptize, teach?

Do you witness; do you testify?

These simple imperatives implanted in the heart of every true believer literally changed the course of human history, rattled the cage of the nations, as the message of the Gospel of Christ Jesus exploded throughout the world. That His message would compel His people today, the Church, to the ends of the earth, the nations.

Even so, we must go further. This is fundamental, but God has much, much more concerning His will for believers.

In my own hand

THOUGH the Book was written in eternity past, the Lord saved me in March of 2005. During our church's Passion Play, He stirred my heart and at the invitation, I raised my hand and surrendered my life to Christ, though I knew He had been performing a work within me for quite some time. In the weeks prior, as the pastor would give the invitation at the end of the service, I would literally hold onto the pew for dear life. I didn't want to surrender, though I knew I must. Through the supernatural regeneration of the Holy Spirit, surrender to Christ was now within my nature. I was bent toward God.

Following salvation, Jesus slowly, assuredly began to take possession of an increasingly larger portion of my life. I became intensely exasperated, frustrated to the point of anger.

"It can't all be about God can it!" I yelled at Ami.

At some point, an interesting situation developed. We joined a Sunday School class and eventually they asked me to teach. The response from the class was overwhelmingly positive. I began to timidly envision myself in a leadership capacity in the church. Could I be a pastor? Maybe this was just my natural inclination to envision myself in charge, no matter the situation? Years of Army training had certainly conditioned my thoughts in this manner.

Yet, the feeling persisted. I found myself finishing our pastor's sermons in my mind as he preached.

I began to know, to *know*, deep in my heart, that God was calling me to preach. He placed a yearning inside of me, a deep and abiding ache. His Word began to burn in my heart like a fire. (Jer. 20:9) Yet, I had a problem.

I was an active duty Army officer with over ten years of active duty service at the time. At some point, we studied Abraham who *went,* not knowing where the Lord was leading him, but he went. I anguished. I despaired.

What did God want me to do?

Am I supposed to get out of the Army immediately?

How will I feed my family?

Where is my faith?

As I tore myself apart, the Lord waited patiently. Finally, I could contain myself no longer and so I *planned* ahead that during the following Sunday evening service, I would go forward at the invitation and declare God's call to preach because obviously, all spiritual decisions must be made at a church-wide invitation, or else they just aren't valid.

So there I sat that Sunday evening, in agony. As the pastor delivered the invitation, he asked if any wanted to *decide* for Christ. Did any feel God's call to repent and believe?

"Perhaps someone needs to make another spiritual decision," he asked.

My heart froze in my chest. My breathing became laborious. I'm sure I broke into a sweat. This was it, the moment of truth. I prepared to rise and go forward when I looked down at my attire and noticed I was clad in shorts and a T-shirt.

I couldn't go forward looking like this!

It just wouldn't be right.

I had an out and that was all I needed. Deflated, I left quietly and went home.

The following week, I entered the church dejected. I had failed. I hardly heard the sermon and again, the pastor got to the invitation and this time, I remember it like yesterday, he specifically asked,

"Perhaps someone here feels led to surrender into ministry."

With a jolt, my cell phone started vibrating loudly in my pocket. God had called me! [Later I would learn it was just work, but I have no doubt that it was God] As if in a dream or a daze, I rose and went forward to our pastor, who is a spiritual hero of mine, and in tears I told him that I didn't know what it meant and that I didn't know any details, but that I had to surrender to this call to preach the Word of God. I couldn't agonize over the details one second longer. He hugged me and presented me to the church and the congregation responded overwhelmingly. It was almost as if they had been waiting on me this entire time.

"What of the Army?" you may ask.

Nearly nine years later, I still serve in the Army and I preach the Word of God. There are days whereby I pray for God to grant me release from the Army, usually when I am rolling out of bed at 4:30 in the morning, but God, in His infinite and unsearchable wisdom, has entrusted to me a vast ministry in a dark and restless place, the hearts of countless young Soldiers.

My most discerning and beautiful wife Ami pointed this fact out to me some time before.

"You are surrounded by and have great influence over vast quantities of young men who don't know Christ!" she exclaimed to me in exasperation. I was waiting for her to add, "you idiot!" because that's how I felt.

I had become paralyzed by inaction whereby God had already equipped me, put me where He wanted me, and illuminated the path. I speak of Christ at work often. Currently I am privileged to command nearly 700 soldiers. I also serve bi-vocationally as the Missions Pastor at a local church where I am privileged to proclaim the Gospel, to preach. I still await my release from active duty.

"What of the Army?" you ask of me?

"What is that in your hand?" I ask of you.

Then Moses answered, "What if they won't believe me and will not obey me but say, 'The LORD did not appear to you'?"

The LORD asked him, "What is that in your hand?"

"A staff," he replied.

Exodus 4:1,2

The voice of the LORD spoke loud and clear from the burning bush, commissioning Moses to lead God's people. Yet, he doubted. "Who am I?" he asks. (Ex. 3:12) How could I possibly be the one to lead the people? What if they don't listen to me? What if they don't believe me?

What is that in your hand?

A staff?

God makes the point to Moses that He has already equipped him for whatever He has called him to do. It is not as if God whimsically decided to give Moses a try. In eternity past, God ordained Moses to lead His people and God equipped Him for the path to which He called him, in this case, with a staff, a staff that he already possessed.

Believers, you are already equipped. You already have the tools, the means, and the capacity to do what God is willing for you to do at this particular point. Paul expounds on this very point,

However, each one must live his life in the situation the Lord assigned when God called him... Each person should remain in the life situation in which he was called... Brothers, each person should remain with God in whatever situation he was called.

1 Corinthians 7:17,20,24

God has placed you in your current life position for a reason and He has equipped you for the work to which He has called you. Too often, believers think that they must go forth and complete some amazing task for the Lord or else they aren't serving. Where has the Lord placed you in your life? **Do your neighbors know the Lord? Your friends? Your children?**

God has equipped and will equip each and every one of us to walk the path He would have us walk and that we are currently walking. He has placed us in our respective lives intentionally, deliberately. Open your eyes. Look. See. At some point, it becomes too obvious to ignore.

What is that in your hand? Examine your grasp and I think you'll be surprised at what you actually hold.

First Things

LEST we should forget the primacy of God's mission for our lives, Jesus exhorts us,

But seek first the kingdom of God and His righteousness, and all these things will be provided for you.

Matthew 6:33

In serving God, my attitude and focus require much examination, seeking the alignment of my goals and objectives with His. As the natural man – needs, desires, and wants – clings to our spirit, competing with the Higher Calling, the calling that renders unto eternity vice the temporal outworking of the flesh, God urges us to forsake all for the Kingdom of God, the Kingdom referring to the existing and continual rule of the one true God.

As the believer anxiously frets about the trivial and miniscule, the Kingdom of God steadily advances. Won't you be a part of it? Step forward, raise your hand. God will handle the details of our daily existence. Make your attitude one of reflection of the primacy of the Kingdom of God. Concern yourself not with the details of daily existence. Will not the Lord provide?

Look at the birds of the sky: they don't sow or reap or gather into barns, yet your heavenly Father feeds them. Aren't you worth more than they? Can any of you add a single cubit to his height by worrying? And why do you worry about clothes? Learn how the wildflowers grow: they don't labor or spin thread. Yet I tell you that not even Solomon in all his splendor was adorned like one of these

Matthew 6:26-29

In opposition to many common thought patterns amongst supposed professing believers and those who would otherwise preach His word, God's primary call to the believer is not to prosperity or happiness. These are secondary in the economy of God. Quite the contrary, God calls believers to holiness, to live lives of purity, to be sanctified, set apart from the world and all that it represents in opposition to God.

God calls believers to be different, to live differently and it starts with personal holiness. **God is infinitely more concerned with our holiness than with our happiness.** The theme of personal holiness permeates the Word of God.

"What am I to do?" you may still ask. Peter provides an answer:

Be holy, because I am holy.
1 Peter 1:16

The words of the Lord are strikingly simple. Be holy. God commands holiness. Those who seek want the Grand Plan. They want the blueprint. They desire the burning bush all the while ignoring this veritable shout from the smoldering thicket. Be holy.

What am I to do?

Be holy.

An overseas missionary visited our church not too long ago. This was the first time he and his family had visited the country in several years and they eagerly shared their testimony. At the conclusion, we sought to pray for him and we asked what his specific prayer needs were. Interestingly enough, they had just recently lost some financing and so he had obvious concerns about feeding his family of six. As such, I certainly expected him to request our prayers in that regard. As he spoke, he mentioned the finances and the needs of his congregation in Peru but he said that, in spite of these, he was feeling convicted for us to pray for his personal holiness.

This struck me. Here was a man, a committed missionary of the Lord, proclaiming the Gospel in a faraway land and his primary prayer request was for holiness.

"Be holy as I am holy."

Peter didn't invent this command or receive any new revelation here as he quotes from the Old Testament book of Leviticus.

Many seeking to undermine the veracity of Scripture point to the characteristically odd practices described in great detail in this unusual book. Yet, most miss the hermeneutically derived themes of holiness and purity that pervade Leviticus focusing on the *what* versus the *why*.

Why must the priest go to such remarkable lengths to purify himself prior to presenting any of the sacrifices? God considers our sin infinitely more seriously than any of us do. Thus, one cannot approach God in his natural state; he must be purified in some way. The holiness of the one making sacrifices for atonement is infinitely important in the eyes of God.

They [priests] are to be holy to their God and not profane the name of their God…
They [priests] must be holy…
He [the priest] will be holy to you because I, the LORD who sets you apart, am holy…

Leviticus 21:6,8b

Likewise, the people must be purified and holy prior to fellowship with the community of God's people. God desires that His people exist together in holiness that glorifies God. The remarkable lengths described in Leviticus all speak to holiness and God's desire that His people live in purity. The seemingly unusual practices are not the point. Holiness is the point.

For I am the LORD your God, so you must consecrate yourselves and be holy because I am holy... For I am the LORD, who brought you up from the land of Egypt to be your God, so you must be holy because I am holy.

Leviticus 11:44-45

The LORD spoke to Moses: "Speak to the entire Israelite community and tell them: Be holy because I, the LORD your God, am holy."

Leviticus 19:1,2

You are to be holy to Me because I, the LORD, am holy, and I have set you apart from the nations to be Mine.

Leviticus 20:26

Paul frequently speaks to the notion of personal holiness,

For this is God's will, your sanctification: that you abstain from sexual immorality, so that each of you knows how to possess his own vessel in sanctification and honor, not with lustful desires, like the Gentiles who don't know God.

1 Thessalonians 4:3-5

Paul states it definitively. This is God's will, that you are holy, sanctified, abstaining from things like sexual immorality that the Gentiles, *who don't know God*, partake in. Again, brothers and sisters, don't complicate matters. God has spoken quite clearly. Be holy as He is holy. Make this a focus of your walk and a quite interesting condition will develop.

Do not be conformed to this age, but be transformed by the renewing of your mind, so that you may discern what is the good, pleasing, and perfect will of God.

Romans 12:2

Paul urges believers to non-conformity and I think you'll find, upon examination, that nothing conforms less to the world than holiness. Holiness stands in complete opposition to all that the world would offer but look closer. *Why* does Paul so urge believers to seek holiness? So that they may discern the will of God, the "good, pleasing, and perfect" will of God. Our discernment is a direct reflection of our holiness and it makes sense.

Believer, if you persist in cluttering your mind and heart with things that are not of God, what would lead you to think that you might be perceptive to the things of God? The more impurities you remove from your daily existence and the more you immerse yourself in the things of God, the more of God you will become. Pursue holiness; discernment will follow. Paul reminds Timothy,

So if anyone purifies himself from these things [what is dishonorable], he will be a special instrument, set apart, useful to the Master, prepared for every good work.

2 Timothy 2:21

As we've considered how you should feel, how you should think, what you ought to pursue regarding the will of God, you may still be asking, *But what must I do?*

As always, God's Word speaks directly to our hearts

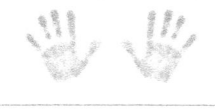

Other Things

AS you, O Believer, pursue first things - the Kingdom of God, holiness - your faith will become tangible, visible even. It will begin to have legs.

Rejoice always!
Pray constantly.
Give thanks in everything,
for this is God's will for you in Christ Jesus.

1 Thessalonians 5:16-18

The Bible calls us to live lives of joy. God has blessed us infinitely with salvation, if nothing else. We have fellowship, through no action or merit of our own, with the one true God, the Creator. We have eternal fellowship, an unbreakable promise of redemption present and redemption continual. How can we not rejoice?

We have access to God. As one of the redeemed, I have no need for a priest or any other intercessor. Christ is my intercessor and indeed, He has already made intercession for me. He continually intercedes for me. How can I not continually seek the counsel of the Father?

In all of these, access and blessings, we are to live lives of humble thankfulness, in everything.

Prayer, joy, and thanksgiving ought to permeate every aspect of our existence. We ought to have continual fellowship with the Father.

Don't reserve your prayers for the church building or the designated place or time of day. What of those who suffer? Notice the Bible makes no stipulation for conditions. Rejoice *if,* pray *if*, give thanks *if*. No. The Bible tells us to live continually in these things and if you suffer, fashion yourself after the fathers,

After they called for the apostles and had them flogged, they ordered them not to speak in the name of Jesus and released them. Then they went out from the presence of the Sanhedrin, rejoicing that they were counted worthy to be dishonored on behalf of the name.

Acts 5:40-41

Did you catch that? The apostles considered it a matter of great joy that they were counted worthy to suffer on behalf of Jesus and they gave thanks in their affliction. As Polycarp, disciple of John, went to the fire, he thanked God that He counted him worthy to be numbered among the martyrs. This very spirit prompted Origen to exclaim, "What greater joy there can be than the act of martyrdom!"

An Unpopular Call

OUR faith must resonate in our relationships.

The true Christian lives a life of submission. Contemporary thought considers this notion of submission as anathema to how things actually should be. It is a dirty word, tied closely to subordination and subjugation. The heathen will certainly look incredulously upon those who acknowledge and even endorse the biblical call of submission and certainly many believers as well.

Many in the church have attempted to soften the concept and

repeatedly emphasize misconceived notions of mutual submission or spend vast amounts of time emphasizing the contrary side of the submissive relationship as if God's call for people to submit is something that should be minimized. Many seem embarrassed by the idea.

Yet, the Bible calls *all* to submit in one way or another and as always, our Lord Jesus provides the greatest example and the Apostle Paul calls us to emulate Him.

> *Make your own attitude that of Christ Jesus,*
> *who, existing in the form*
> *of God, did not consider*
> *equality with God*
> *as something to be used*
> *for His own advantage.*
> *Instead He emptied Himself*
> *by assuming the form*
> *of a slave,*
> *taking on the likeness of men.*
> *He humbled Himself*
> *by becoming obedient*
> *to the point of death –*
> *even to the death on a cross.*

Philippians 2:5-7, 8

Did you catch that? Jesus did not consider equality with God – He was and is, equal with God – as something to be used for advantage, something He very easily could have done as He mentions at Gethsemane,

> *Or do you not think that I cannot call on My Father, and He will provide Me at once with more than 12 legions of angels.*

Matthew 26:53

No, in all of this, the Son submitted willingly to the Father. His example of submission, submission by the infinite, provides our highest example. The Bible calls all believers to submit along these lines.

The Bible calls all believers to exist under headship within the church in submitting to the elders,

Obey your leaders and submit to them, for they keep watch over your souls...

Hebrews 13:17a

to the government,

Everyone must submit to the governing authorities, for there is no authority except from God, and those that exist are instituted by God.

Romans 13:1

and to one another in various forms. It is interesting that Paul spends three chapters (Ephesians 1-3) describing salvation through faith and grace alone, not by works so that no man may boast (Ephesians 2:8) and then spends three chapters describing the natural outworking of that faith.

Paul says, here is faith and then, because you have faith, here are some natural ramifications, and of these three chapters, he uses nearly a third of the text explaining relationships and the notion of submission within these various relationships. He first urges believers to, "give thanks always" (Eph. 5:20) – sound familiar – followed closely with this admonishment as a modifying participle phrase, *submitting to one another in the fear of the Christ.*

Ephesians 5:21

Many have taken this to mean that all Christians submit to one another, but Paul explains what he actually means as he proceeds to describe three separate types of submission,

Wives, submit to your own husbands as to the Lord. (v. 22)

Now as the church submits to Christ, so wives should submit to their husband in everything. (v. 24)

Children, obey your parent in the Lord, because this is right. (v. 6:1)

Slaves, obey your human masters with fear and trembling, in the sincerity of your heart, as to Christ. (v. 5)

Paul says submit to one another and here's how. Wives, submit to your husbands. Children, submit to your parents. Slaves, submit to your masters. Now, I do not intend to give a detailed exegesis and rationale as to why God gives these commands but clearly this is God's will. It is of God. It is right.

Just for clarity sake, the man is afforded an equally, if not more profoundly important task,

Husbands, love your wives, just as also Christ loved the church and gave Himself for her, (v. 5:25)

In the same way, husbands should love their wives as their own bodies. (v. 28)

And fathers, don't stir up anger in your children, but bring them up in the training and instruction of the Lord. (v. 6:4)

The implications of these three simple verses are uniquely infinite and uniquely masculine. The man is called to be the spiritual leader of the home as Christ leads the church and God calls wives to submit to husbands, children to submit to parents, and slaves to submit to masters.

Again, notice that the Word makes no concessions for worth. Notice what the Word does not say. It does not say submit to your husband, if he is worthy of being submitted to. It doesn't say love your wife as Christ loved the church, if she is worthy of this love. It doesn't say, submit to your parents until you get older and figure out that you know more than they.

The implications of these commands, of the will of God, to submit, are staggering in their implications. What is God's will for your life? I can say very clearly that God is calling you to live as He would have you live in the ordered relationships. If you are a wife, God is calling you to submit. If you have parents, God is calling you to submit. If you have a wife, God is calling you to love her uniquely as Christ loves the church. That we all would heed this simple yet profound call.

Multiplicity

THE tangible aspect of faith resonates in the very notion of the *stewardship of life*.

To the garden we must return in order to examine this aspect of God's will for man. As God completed His creation, He presented Eve to Adam and he exclaimed, "This one at last is bone of my bone and flesh of my flesh." (Genesis 2:23) The author goes on to explain that, "this is why a man leaves his father and mother and bonds with his wife, and they become one flesh." (Genesis 2:24) The reason that a man leaves his parents and bonds with his wife is that she exists. She is the reason. God gave man the reason, woman, and he is to bond with her and two are to become one flesh.

Back to chapter one where God gives his first recorded command to the *couple*,

> *God blessed them, and God said to them, "Be fruitful, multiply, fill the earth, and subdue it."*
>
> Genesis 1:28a

God is commanding Adam to know his wife Eve in the strictest biblical sense of the word and to have children and to raise them up in the Lord's ways. This is how, prior to the Fall, God's people were to populate the earth, not through evangelism. Adam and Eve, as they already lived in fellowship with God, didn't need evangelizing nor should their children have needed it.

This notion is not void, even in today's fallen world that groans under the very weight of its sin and affliction. In addressing the issue of divorce and the importance of marriage, Jesus returns to Genesis,

> *and He also said:*
> *For this reason a man*
> *will leave*
> *his father and mother*
> *and be joined to his wife,*
> *and the two will become*
> *one flesh?*
>
> Matthew 19:5

Further, Jesus stated that, "what God has joined together, man must not separate." (vs. 6b) Jesus emphasized the critical importance of marriage and not for the self-satisfaction of the individual, but as a physical depiction of Christ and the Church and the Bible repeatedly speaks, post-Fall, of the need to raise up godly children.

*Teach a youth about the way
he should go;
even when he is old
he will not depart from it.*

Proverbs 22:6

The author is speaking directly to the responsibility of parents to teach their children about the ways of the Lord. Deuteronomy chapter six records the giving of the great *Shem'a*. "Hear O' Israel the LORD our God, the LORD is One." (Deuteronomy 6:4) Immediately following this great declaration of faith, the Word says:

Repeat them [these words] to your children.

Deuteronomy 6:7a

Herein lies this great statement of faith but God did not intend it solely for you. You must repeat it to your children, always. "Talk about it", Scripture says. (v. 7b) "Write them on your doorposts." (v. 9) "Bind them on your hand... and on your forehead." (v. 8)

God requires that we teach these great truths to our children that we bring them up in godly ways. All this is not to impugn the gift of singleness. Some are chosen for this specific call, but in general, God calls His people to marry, have children, and disciple the children, raising them up in the ways of the Lord.

The onus lies upon the parents, not the church or the youth pastor, but the parents. Scripture does not abrogate the call of God from the Garden to be fruitful and multiply. God wills that men and women marry, have children, and raise them as disciples of Christ Jesus, to acceptably steward the most precious of commodities, human life.

A More Exacting Call

This life hangs in the balance, quite literally. The situation is intensely more desperate than most realize. Daily, countless numbers march to their demise apart from our Lord, destined for eternal suffering. The wretched dregs exist in the here and now, unlovable and quite unloved. What will you do?

Are you ready, at this point, to hear this most exacting call? Are you strong enough? In Christ, are you strong enough? And so I come to you with this most urgent of pleas. Unfortunately, we don't have much time.

But what does God want me to do?

Amazingly, you may still be asking this question and I urge you to reconsider.

Do you really want to know the answer to this question?

I seek to address this query from the pages of Scripture, though you may not want to hear the answer. As a matter of fact, I can say resolutely that many will not want to hear what Scripture has to say. Many will even *oppose* what I am to about present to you.

As such, if you do not want to be challenged, I urge you to put this work down now and walk away. Read no further. If you do not want to be called out of your most comfortable of existences, then I strongly urge you to stop reading immediately.

As it is, the cry of the Orphan resonates from the pages of Scripture. The Orphan maintains a distinctly special place in the heart of the Lord. In some aspects, the Orphan *is* Jesus, the Orphan embodies the very person of Christ. If you want to see Jesus, look no further than your local orphanage.

Believer, never forget your own fatherlessness prior to your heavenly Father calling you out of the darkness and into his marvelous light. God holds adoption as a decidedly sacred institution. As such, it requires examination, demands it even. Just what does God say about adoption, about the Orphan?

The following pages will address this call that God has placed on the hearts and minds of every believer, though most walk away or ignore it. Some consider it important, just not for them.

For those who are curious or committed, I pray fervently that you'll consider what I am about to tell you, indeed, what God has already told us. Actually, for honesty's sake, I am praying that the Holy Spirit will convict your collective hearts when it comes to this particular call and you'll believe me that…

…there is *No Higher Call.*

> LORD, You have heard the desire of the humble;
> You will prepare their heart;
> You will cause Your ear to hear,
> To do justice to the fatherless and the oppressed,
> That the man of the earth may oppress no more.
>
> Psalm 10:17-18 (NKJV)

QUESTIONS

1. Review 2 Timothy 3:16,17.

    a. What is the context of Paul's statement to Timothy? Examine the surrounding text in chapter 3.

    b. Why did Paul make this statement at this particular point in the letter?

    c. What do these verses tell us about the sufficiency of Scripture?

    d. Where do most people look for answers, or even yourself? Why is this?

2. Read Colossians 3:23 again.

    a. Paul literally states to do things "from the soul". What does he mean by this?

    b. How can we do things "from the soul" in our daily existence?

    c. What would this look like in the various aspects of our lives? How might this affect ourselves, our families, our nation?

3. Matthew 6:33 defines priorities for a Christian life. Discuss the application of Jesus' statement. How well do you apply this? How well does your church apply this? What inhibits the application of this?

4. Reread Acts 5:40-41. How could the Apostles rejoice in this manner? Do you know any who have "suffered on behalf of the name"? What do you fear? Why does this fear resonate? What does this passage tell us about fear and suffering?

5. This chapter discusses general insight on the will of God. What particular aspect stood out to you? Is there an element you struggle with? Of the three types of believers mentioned in the first part of the chapter, which are you?

> Learn to do good;
> Seek justice,
> Rebuke the oppressor;
> Defend the fatherless,
> Plead for the widow.
>
> Isaiah 1:17 (NKJV)

CHAPTER 3

IT has occurred to me that speaking on behalf of God is an intensely serious business. I must remind myself that some will most assuredly become unhappy when confronted with God's Word in general, but certainly as it pertains to the Orphan. God's Word will always divide, always convict, never returning void.

If I told you that God wanted you to be happy, or that God intended you to prosper financially, perhaps that would appease your spirit. If I told you God has wonderful plans for your life, that would almost certainly please you as well.

Yet, what if I were to tell you that God intended for you to suffer, that Jesus assures His followers of persecution in His name? What if I told you that God actually honored suffering on behalf of the Name? What if I informed you that God had called you to something *lesser*? What if I relayed to you that God intended you to languish in penury? I didn't say these things, but if I did, would you react differently? Would praises fall from your lips as readily as when the call of God yields comfort and prosperity?

As I reflect upon my lack of desire to ever rear children, it occurred to me that an increasing number of westerners are having fewer children with many choosing never to have any at all. What would have been unthinkable as recently as a couple of decades ago has become normative. I know many adult couples who have no children, nor do they intend to ever raise a family.

It also occurred to me that many couples cannot have children; they are unable, physiologically speaking.

A Bruised Heel

AS you consider these things with respect to the Orphan, we must return to the Garden, to the first preaching of the Gospel. **We must draw the foundation of our conclusions from the foundation of *all* things.**

Genesis chapter 3, a single chapter that, if torn from the pages of the Bible would certainly render the entire body of Scripture irrelevant, contains the account of the Fall. Eve and Adam rebelled against God, Eve first, though God and the pages of Scripture hold Adam entirely responsible (Rom. 5:12-21) as it is the trespass of one *man* that brought sin and death into the world demanding the atoning sacrifice of a second *Adam*.

The man and woman, cowering in the bushes, represent all that humanity would now become. God addresses them both and then the Curse. Curiously, God addresses Satan first, "that ancient serpent, who is the Devil and Satan." (Rev. 20:2)

> *I will put hostility between you*
> *and the woman,*
> *and between your seed*
> *and her seed.*
> *He will strike your head,*
> *and you will strike [bruise] his heel.*

Genesis 3:15

The *protoevangelium*, literally the first Gospel, announces God's glorious intentions for the first time, the revelation of a plan ordained in eternity past. That the seed of the woman, Jesus, would crush the head of Satan, destroying him, is a forgone, *public* conclusion from this point forward, actualized at Calvary, to be consummated at the *Parousia*. Yet the bruised heel demands consideration with respect to the Orphan. This heel of the Seed, bruised, and stricken by the Serpent, demands examination.

As it was...

THE two preceding chapters, Genesis 1 and 2, give a picture of things as they were, perfect as God intended. God created everything in six literal days and when He had finished, He gathered together the dust of the ground and formed man, breathing the *pneuma*, the *ruach* of life into his very lungs.

God gave man authority. He taught man. He issued man the ordinance of work, tending the Garden, a holy work similar to the later work of the Levites in caring for the Tabernacle.

Then, when all of creation was completed, perfect, prepared, ready, God created woman. He saw that it was not good for man to be alone and so while he slept, He took a rib from the man and made woman and when he awoke, he presented woman to man and the man exclaimed, "This one at last is bone of my bone and flesh of my flesh" and moreover, "this is why a man leaves his father and mother and bonds with his wife, and they become one flesh." (Gen. 2:24) A man leaves his parents because of woman. She *is* the reason.

God saw all that He had created and it was *very* good. (Gen. 1:31)

Returning to chapter 1, a parallel but distinct account from chapter 2, we'll find God's first command to the *couple*. "Be fruitful, multiply, fill the earth, and subdue it." (Gen. 1:28) God commanded Adam to *know* his wife Eve in the strictest biblical sense of the word, to have children and by implication and assumption, to bring them up in the way of the Lord. This is the way that God's people were to populate the earth. Evangelism did not yet exist, nor did a requirement for evangelism exist. The created order and the commands of God imply discipleship between parent and child.

Perfect harmony resonated over all of creation: harmony between God and man, between man and Creation, between man and woman. The natural progression assumes and implies the foregone conclusion of intended harmony between parent and child.

Genesis 1 and 2 provide a useful glimpse of the way things were.

As it should be...

THE idea of how things were does not ring hollow today. The existence of the Fall does not render pre-Fall conditions as irrelevant. Recency does not necessarily abrogate previous ordinances. No, the conditions, the harmony presented in Genesis 1 and 2, provide a unique prism through which to view the idea of how things should be. When we consider children in general – disregard the Orphan for the time being – the harmony resonant pre-Fall provides a view, a picture, that will certainly lend insight into how things ought to be.

Certainly great humor exists in talking about children in a certain way. The comedian Bill Cosby frequently expounded upon life with a large family and I remember one particular set where he spoke to the need to, "get the children OUT of the house. He wants them OUT of the house!" punctuating each utterance with a dramatic thrust of his finger and a pained facial expression. *My wife was a beautiful woman... and then the children came...*

Many comically lament the impact of children upon a couple's sex life. I, myself, frequently joke – sort of – that I don't even really like children. I can rather confidently assert that God must possess an amazing sense of humor or irony, or perhaps both.

Yet, all kidding aside, the Bible speaks about children in a decidedly different manner.

> *Sons are indeed a heritage*
> *from the LORD,*
> *children, a reward.*
> *Like arrows in the hand*
> *of a warrior*
> *are the sons born in*
> *one's youth.*
>
> Psalms 127:3-4

The Word tells us that sons, children, are a heritage from the LORD, literally an inheritance, a cherished possession. Most would consider it good to inherit something, be it wealth or property and generally speaking, the one who bequeaths, the one who passes whatever it is down, usually calls upon whoever he gives this particular thing to, to take care of it, to be a steward of it, to treasure it. Typically, most will only pass something down to someone, be it family members or friends, who will cherish the item as they have.

In this same way, God has designated sons, children, as a heritage. Where do children come from? They come from the LORD, and He blesses people with them. He passes them down. He entrusts people with them. Children are a heritage and more than that, God calls them a reward.

This entire notion amplifies the value of children, the value that the LORD places upon them. The idea of a reward implies something given to you in recognition of your service or achievement, something honorable, something of value.

Children are not a burden. Children are not a hindrance. Children are not a nuisance or an impediment to your own personal happiness and satisfaction. Children are a *heritage* from the LORD. They are a *reward* from the LORD.

Children possess intrinsic value in the eyes of the LORD. **Children have great value in the eyes of the LORD.**

Further, from Psalm 127, children serve as a weapon. Ephesians chapter 6 tells us that our enemy is not the flesh and blood, but the rulers, the authorities, the world powers of this darkness, the spiritual forces of evil in the heavens. (Eph. 6:12) The Bible tells us "to stand against the tactics of the Devil". (v. 11) We read that a vast spiritual battle for the souls of all mankind rages around us every single day and that children serve as weapons in this battle. They are "like arrows in the hand of a warrior". The rub here is that you actually have to be a warrior to wield a weapon and I would certainly argue that God through His Word calls all Christians to fight as warriors in this epic struggle.

Ephesians gives us the Word of God, that is the Sword of the Spirit, (v. 17) as our weapon in this war and here in the Psalms, the Word tells us that children, sons, are like arrows in the hands of a warrior.

Think of an arrow. If unfired, it has not fulfilled its purpose. An arrow must be fired. To be effective, it must be *aimed*. This implies intentionality, training perhaps.

The Psalmist continues, "Happy is the man who has filled his quiver with them". (Ps. 127:5) The Psalmist equates happiness, blessedness, with a full quiver. A man with many children, a man with many sons, has certainly been blessed by the LORD, favored by God.

Years ago, this attitude pervaded culture. The more children you had, the more blessed you were, the happier you were. Children meant more hands to help out around the farm or the home. Sons meant more people to carry on the family name. Children meant more people to take care of you as you got older. Children meant more people for you to raise in a godly way, but today, in the self-absorbed culture of the west, the culture of *me*, people see children as a hindrance to their careers or even a hindrance to their personal social lives.

Did you know that in many parts of the world, governments have necessarily instituted campaigns to encourage people to have children? In Russia, for example, as the population has aged and become increasingly self-absorbed, having fewer and fewer children, the government is offering incentives for couples to reproduce. Similar conditions exist elsewhere, in Iran for example.

Yet, the LORD has a view of children that runs counter to the pervading secular view of children. In the LORD's opinion, the only opinion with merit, children have value, extreme value. They are a heritage, a reward, a weapon in this war many so unwillingly wage.

As it should be (continued)...

IN light of this curious idea that children can serve as weapons in this great spiritual battle to which God calls us all, we see that the Bible repeatedly calls for parents, fathers really, but parents to raise their children in godly ways. Deuteronomy 6:4 records the *Shem'a*, the great statement of the foundation of the Abrahamic faith. "Hear O' Israel the LORD our God, the LORD is one." Immediately following this, Moses reminds us that, *these words that I am giving you today are to be in your heart. Repeat them to your children.*

Deuteronomy 6:6-7b

Parents are to repeat these words of faith to their children, daily, constantly. Further,

Teach a youth about the way he should go; even when he is old he will not depart from it.

Proverbs 22:6

We can easily see reflections of Genesis 1, "Be fruitful, multiply, fill the earth with God's people." The Fall did not render these commands null, abrogated. As we saw in Psalm 127, children have great value as a heritage, a reward, a weapon. Teach them the ways of the LORD, and when they grow older, they will certainly not depart from them. I am often intensely amazed at how quickly children take to Jesus.

We have, in our family, a little Mexican guy named Juan Miguel. At nearly four years of age, Juan Miguel has lived with us for nearly two years and he is bad! And I do mean bad! And we love it!

Juan Miguel received absolutely no discipline previously. He would hit kids, take their things, throw fits. You name it. So we instantly set about correcting his behavior.

In addition to his discipline, we ensured he received and continues to receive a healthy dose of Jesus. Every night, when I tuck Juan in, we pray for Jesus to forgive him of his sins – quite extensive I might add, but hey, who's perfect. He puts his little hands together and in his little voice, prays to Jesus and guess what? When I am in a rush, or it's late, or I am just being a slacker and try to skip out on praying, he won't let me. He actually gets upset if I try to put him to bed without praying to Jesus.

This is how it should be. This is how things ought to be.

Many fail to realize that the issue of the Orphan is a Gospel issue. Did you know that statistically speaking, no adults convert to Christianity? Adult converts do not exist. Now, obviously exceptions exist. As an adult convert myself, I can testify to that, but in general, if a child leaves the home unsaved, **he will likely die unsaved.** Very few adult converts exist as most inherit at a young age the faith or lack thereof, of their *fathers*.

Even secular sociologists acknowledge that the number one influence in a child's life is his parents, his father really, but his parents… whether you are present, what you teach, how you act, what you say… whether you are absent, what you don't teach, what you don't say. Either way, parents, fathers, but parents provide the greatest influence in a child's life.

This conclusion, the absolutely essential nature of the influence of a parent, brings us to the next condition we must assess, how things actually are.

As it is…

LET us consider for a moment, the reality of life, the reality of this existence. We've examined how it was, how it should be. Let's examine the reality of how things actually are, how it is.

Let's revisit the *protoevangelium*. This happens as a result of the Fall of man, the Original Sin of the first Adam. God curses Satan. God curses man and woman. Creation is cursed.

The Fall shattered the universal harmony that had permeated the fabric of all things and replaced that harmony with struggle and strife.

Discord replaces harmony between God and man.

Discord reigns between man and creation.

Discord supplants harmony between man and woman.

Now *anticipated* discord – actualized today but anticipated then – replaces harmony between parent and child. The notion of godly parents raising children in the LORD's ways and populating the earth with His people in this fashion has been replaced by this same struggle and strife that now epitomizes the relationships between God and man, man and creation, and man and woman.

The Fall shattered harmony. Satan will bruise or strike the heel of Christ.

Let's consider the heel of Christ from Genesis 3:15.

A *temporal* bruising of Jesus' heel occurred at Calvary. Almost every theologian will acknowledge this as a foretold aspect of the bruised heel of the *protoevangelium*. Evil men driven by Satan intended to destroy Jesus at Calvary. On the cross, Satan truly believed he had defeated Christ, but what we see is our God fashioning the will of men and even the will of Satan to accomplish His purposes. God intended the cross all along. Satan, though complicit, acted unwitting to this. Yet, Christ was wounded, the bruising of His heel.

Upon the cross, Jesus bore the physical pain of crucifixion, the unimaginable pain as the Roman soldiers nailed Him to the cross. He bore the pain of the scourging prior to crucifixion. He bore the anguish of rejection by His people as the same folks who were shouting, "Hosanna! Hosanna in the highest!" just a week before, were now shouting, "Crucify Him!" before the Sanhedrin and Pilate. Jesus bore this pain of betrayal.

Yet, most of all, He bore the wrath of a righteous and holy God for the sins of mankind. He bore the full fury and wrath of God Almighty in all of His justifiable rage against the sin of the created as they rebelled against the Creator.

Satan certainly bruised the figurative heel of Christ at Calvary, temporally.

As Christ hung dying on the cross, bloodied and naked, He turned his gaze heavenward and exclaimed, *"Elí, Elí, lemá sabachtháni?"* that is, "My God, My God, why have You forsaken Me?" (Matthew 27:46) Some have referenced this statement and erroneously contrived a *forsaken* Jesus or an *abandoned* Jesus, a *pitiable* Jesus. That is, as He became sin for us, the Father could not help but turn His back on the Son.

However, nothing could be further from the truth. Jesus is, in fact, quoting Psalm 22, a Messianic psalm, a psalm of trust, a psalm the attending religious leaders would have recognized instantly. In essence, Jesus is declaring His Messiah-ship from the cross and His trust in the perfect plan of the Father. The Father loves the Son with a perfect love that can never and has never been broken.

As such, let us now consider another aspect of this bruising of Christ's heel. In this, we must consider the heart of God. Let us reflect upon the perfect love of God. "God is love." (1 John 4:16) God loves people, His creation (Ps. 9) and He possesses a special love for His people.

God is immutable, transcendent, impassible. He does not change; He is completely separate from His creation, uncreated; He is not defined by emotion, incapable of suffering. Yet, in His unsearchable ways and existence, we see frequently an indicator of the heart of God, specifically when speaking about the betrayal of His people.

The Old Testament prophets called His people to repentance time and time again and God, in His wrath, casts judgment. Yet, examine the language of Hosea, immediately after the prophet pronounces judgment upon the people,

> *How can I give you up, Ephraim? How can I surrender you, Israel? How can I make you like Admah? How can I treat you like Zeboiim? I have had a change of heart; My compassion is stirred!*

Hosea 11:8

His people have rejected Him, repeatedly, consistently, and still His heart moves to mercy. Still His heart moves to compassion. God loves people. God loves *His* people. The language indicates that judgment upon them brings Him anguish.

Moreover, God loves children. Jesus loves children.

Matthew chapter 21 records children cheering for Jesus and Jesus shames the priests by their praise. Mark 10 records that people actually brought their children to Jesus just to have him touch them. People traveled great distances, enduring hardship, enduring danger, just to give their children to Jesus. Jesus has a special love for children and He even commends the faith of children, their childlike faith in Him.

As we consider the bruising of Christ's heel, his wounding on the cross at Calvary, another application, another way that Satan wounded Christ, and continues to wound Him today, is through the affliction of His people. Satan despises God. Satan loathes God. Satan wants to usurp, to replace God, but Satan cannot harm the Almighty. Yet, what better way to harm God than by afflicting those He loves, people, His people, and children, especially children. This is a *continual* bruising of the heel of Christ.

Today, Satan and the world afflict children greatly. I would argue that children are afflicted today as never before.

Children are beaten;

Children are abused;

Children are neglected;

Children are afflicted from conception, in the womb, by the evil scourge of chemical abuse through the sins and affliction of the mother.

Children are murdered before ever being born at an unprecedented rate, by the tens of millions.

Most of all, children are abandoned and betrayed by the very ones who are supposed to be protecting them, teaching them, loving them, raising them.

Children are afflicted today as never before and perhaps most urgently, *who is going to teach them the Gospel?* With no parents, who is going to bring them up in the ways of the LORD, as it should be?

The affliction of children bruises Jesus' heel. It breaks His heart.

If you have children, you love your children. Now, imagine your anguish if you were to see them suffer, see them in affliction. Maybe you've had to endure that, the suffering of your children, and so you understand this pain. Either way, consider that this anguish originates from the love in a decidedly wicked and sinful human heart.

Now, imagine the pain God, in His infinite and perfect love, must feel at the suffering and affliction of His children. Instead of the temporal bruising of Jesus' heel at Calvary we see the continual bruising of Christ through the affliction of children.

The Bible records the tears of Jesus on several occasions. Jesus wept, as He surveyed his friends outside Lazarus's tomb, bemoaning their lack of understanding. Jesus wept, as he surveyed Jerusalem, lamenting its impending betrayal and judgment.

I can say with utmost confidence that when a parent walks away from a child, Jesus weeps.

When a parent neglects a child, Jesus weeps.

When a parent betrays a child, Jesus weeps.

When a parent abuses a child, Jesus weeps.

When a child has no home, Jesus weeps.

Remember, children are a heritage, a reward, a weapon, like arrows in the hands of a warrior and happy is the man whose quiver is full. As we tread this vast spiritual battleground what we *should* see is the lifeless body of the enemy lying riddled with the arrows fired by godly men. Instead, we see the scattering of broken arrows littering the battlefield, these broken arrows, the intended sons of godly men, cast aside, never even fired, many of them broken into unrecognizable pieces in their affliction.

This is how it is. This is not how it was, nor how it ought to be. This is how it is. The children of this nation are afflicted as never before and so this begs the obvious question, *What are you going to do about it, Church?*

What are you going to do about it, Church?

There it is. This is the question that must be answered, that this work seeks to answer.

Consider that in 2012, state child protective services received 3.3 million reports of violence against children resulting in 251,764 placements in foster care. Consider that in the same year, 23,439 children turned 18 and "aged-out" of the foster system. No family wanted them permanently. Of these 23,439 children whom no one wants, *almost all of them will fail at life.*

Consider that 1 in 5 will become homeless at some point. Less than half will be employed by age 24. Less than 3% will *ever* earn a college degree. Of the young women, 71% will become pregnant out of wedlock by age 21.[4] Many will end up in jail. Many will struggle with chemical addiction.

We, as a society, have failed these children.

We, as a Church, have failed these children.

They have been abandoned, betrayed, by all of us.

Do we really need to say any more? Does this subject bear further discussion?

Dozens of websites chronicle the struggle of Orphans, those who languish in the system available for adoption this very day. Investigate www.adoptuskids.org. Examine the actual faces of the Orphan. Look into their eyes. Hear their words. Listen to their simple and earnest pleas.

As I gaze into the eyes of these children, these children who need homes, children who have been betrayed, I can almost hear the lamentations of our Lord Jesus. This is how it is. This is how things are. However, we naturally progress toward a glimpse of how things could be.

As it could be...

LET me speak with you about hope for a second. Somewhere, right now, in your city, wherever you live right now, a child, a boy, a girl, a toddler, a teenager needs a mother; they need a father... and they have a hope for that mom and for that dad. They *know*, at some point, they come to the knowledge that without that dad, without that mom, *they don't stand a chance...* they don't stand a chance.

---

[4] Rita Soronen, "We are abandoning children in foster care," accessed December 2014, (http://www.cnn.com/2014/04/16/opinion/soronen-foster-children).

Those children who are never adopted possess a distinctly bleak outlook on life. Poverty, jail, homelessness, children from wedlock, drug abuse, and most of all *godlessness*: these are the fruits of a life lived without parents and sadly, the children of these children will likely travel a similar road.

Still, they have a hope. **If not you, then who? If not now, then when?**

With respect to this hope, the notion of adoption is one of the purest of all notions in the Bible. **Have you forgotten that without Christ, you have no Father?** Without Jesus, you have no hope.

> *But when the completion of time came, God sent His Son, born of a woman, born under the law, to redeem those under the law, so that we might receive adoption as sons. And because you are sons, God has sent the Spirit of His Son into our heart, crying, "Abba, Father!" So you are not longer a slave, but a son; and if a son, then an heir through God.*
>
> Galatians 4:4-7

Returning to the *protoevangelium*, the first preaching of the Gospel, we see that God, in His infinite mercy, preaches the first Gospel to the enemy himself. Satan serves as the audience for the first preaching of the Gospel, spoken by the very Author of that astonishing news.

Yes, Satan will bruise Jesus' heel. He will bruise it temporally at Calvary and he will bruise it continually through the affliction of those that God loves, in this case, children. Did you notice though, that God preaches the Gospel before He ever curses woman, man, or creation. God gives the solution to our sin condition before He even declares the resultant manifestation of that sin condition in the following curses.

Jesus will crush Satan's head, defeating him personally and at Calvary, we see exactly that and the bruising, the bruising is a temporary condition that as we see, heals.

In the same way, God has already ordained, already sent, in His mercy, the solution to the suffering of the children, the solution to the affliction of the children. He has called His Church to the cry of the Orphan, to the Call. He has ordained adoption, physical adoption, as one of the purest physical manifestations of the Gospel of Christ Jesus, as one of the purest manifestations of the love of Christ Jesus.

Somewhere, as the child calls out for a father or a mother, he has a hope. Can you imagine the joy if one day, that child could look at you and cry, "*Abba*, Father!"? This is the essence of the Gospel. The issue of adoption, the issue of the Orphan, is a Gospel issue.

O' Believer, cast aside this notion that you must go forth. Cast aside your paralysis. Pray that the Lord would end your apathy, remove the veil, open your eyes. God has placed a mission field in your very city, right in your town, right in your county. The cry of the Orphan rings loud and clear. Won't you respond? Knowing this need, how can you turn a deaf ear? Just because you may turn a deaf ear, doesn't mean the cry of the Orphan rings any less stridently.

> Do not remove the ancient landmark,
> Nor enter the fields of the fatherless;
>
> Proverbs 23:10 (NKJV)

Bradford Smith

Chapter Three Discussion Questions

QUESTIONS

1. Read the *protoevangelium* from Genesis 3:15.

    a. What are the significant aspects of this first proclamation of the Gospel?

    b. Who was the first audience? Is this significant?

    c. Consider the wounding of Christ, the bruising of His heel. Do you agree with this work's view on the matter concerning Satan's assault upon children? Why or why not

2. Read Psalm 33:11 and Malachi 3:6.

    a. What do these verses tell us about God?

    b. *The Westminster Confession of Faith* states that God is "without body, parts, or passions." (2.1) Define impassibility and immutability. Reconcile these concepts with Hosea 11:8. Does God react from emotion?

3. Read aloud the statistics concerning orphaned children from 2012. How do these move you? Why do you think the outlook is so dismal for foster children who are never adopted?

4. This work makes the statement, "We, as a Church, have failed these children." Do you agree with this statement? Why or why not?

5. What are your thoughts on the statement, "the notion of adoption is one of the purest of all notions in the Bible." Why?

6. Why do you think there are so many orphans in the United States? Do you have any personal experience with orphans?

> Open my eyes, that I may see
> Wondrous things from Your law.
>
> Psalm 119:18 (NKJV)

CHAPTER 4

I'D like to discuss faith for a few minutes, actual saving faith, the faith that saves contrasted with the cheap, watered down 'faith' that many are 'saved' into today. The modern version of 'faith' demands nothing from its recipient, imposes no requirements, as it so readily and conveniently imitates the faith of our fathers in form only, yet not in substance. I have come to despise such contemporary expressions of faith. As Dietrich Bonhoeffer so eloquently phrased it,

> *Costly grace is the gospel which must be sought again and again… what has cost God much cannot be cheap for us.*[5]

I stand flummoxed at those who profess an encounter with the living God of the Universe, having been saved from eternal damnation apart from God by the Atonement, and yet bristle at the notion of this *costing* them anything, *requiring* anything of them. The Bible knows nothing of such faith, such easy believism.

Yet, I'll concede that few issues inflame my personal passions more than the issue of the Orphan. We've discussed generalities concerning the will of God for the believer and

---

[5] Dietrich Bonhoeffer, *The Cost of Discipleship*, (Touchstone: New York, 1959), 45.

we've discussed the need as it pertains to the Orphan, but so what?

I can readily acknowledge any number of needs, but that doesn't mean that I am required to address that need. Somewhere right now a church in sub-Saharan Africa is falling apart. Now, perhaps I have the skill to rebuild this particular church and I also possess the necessary funding to fly myself to this particular place. Does that make it my responsibility? Maybe, but not definitively. Is it the same with the Orphan?

Despite my personal convictions and passions, my ultimate goal for this work is to assess what God says about the matter. In the end, it doesn't matter what I say. It doesn't matter how impassioned my rhetoric or how well I may grandstand. It doesn't matter if I can skillfully manipulate you, the reader, with some well-timed tugs on your heartstrings. None of that matters. It is the Word of God that matters. Let's see where this two-edged sword might penetrate.

Things Jesus says...

JESUS issued some fairly profound and inflammatory statements during His earthly ministry. Perhaps most inflammatory was this statement to the Pharisees and some others like it,

Before Abraham was, I am...

John 8:58

Here, Jesus is equating Himself with God before the religious leaders drawing upon the proper name of God, Yahweh, or more appropriately, YHWH. When Moses inquires of God at the burning bush, "If I go to the Israelites and say to them: The God of your fathers has sent me to you, and they ask me, 'What is His name?' what should I tell them?" to which God responds, "I AM WHO I AM. This is what you are to say to the Israelites: I AM has sent me to you." (Exodus 3:13-14)

The religious leaders understood all too well the reference Jesus invoked and the implication as evidenced by their response, "At that, they picked up stones to throw at Him." (John 8:59) They sought to stone him for this answer.

Further, during Jesus' interaction with the rich, young ruler, He tells him,

Sell all that you have and distribute it to the poor...
Luke 18:22

and a few verses later,

For it is easier for a camel to go through the eye of a needle than for a rich person to enter the kingdom of God... (verse 25)

Just as some do today, in Jesus' day, people equated wealth with God's favor. Yet, Jesus urged this wealthy young man to unburden himself with the weight of wealth and made this statement, alluding to the notion that wealth could certainly serve as a stumbling block. Jesus preaches on money quite frequently and as with today, the people do not always respond graciously.

It seems that if a preacher wants to push his congregation's buttons, all he has to do is preach upon what the Bible says about money and he will be sure to generate a reaction. Look at the response of the rich, young ruler to Jesus, "After he heard this, he became extremely sad, because he was very rich," which only served to validate Jesus' point entirely. (v. 23)

Perhaps no sermon, oration, or speech offers as much in the way of profundity as does the Sermon on the Mount. Again, Jesus' words cut across the grain,

Love your enemies and pray for those who persecute you…
Matthew 5:44

The plight of the Jew is well documented in Scripture and their national history encompasses much in the way of foreign domination. They lived as captives for 400 years under the Egyptians. The Assyrians destroyed Israel, the northern kingdom, in 722 B.C. The Babylonians conquered Jerusalem and the southern kingdom in 586 B.C. The Medo-Persian empire dominated the entire area for several hundred years followed by the Greeks under Alexander the Great. After his death, the Seleucid Empire dominated the portion of the former Greek empire that contained Israel. Following a brief period of independence under the Maccabees, the Roman empire conquered and ruled all of the known world. The Jews lived under the yoke of foreign rule and occupation for millennia and yet, here Jesus tells them to love their enemies. Even the writers of the Psalms, the imprecatory ones anyway, may have taken issue with these words of Jesus.

The book of John records a lengthy series of instruction given by Jesus after the Last Supper whereby He issues this startling statement,

If you love Me, you will keep My commandments…
John 14:15

Perhaps no other statement confronts the Believer in quite the same way as this one. Strikingly simple, it draws a distinct line in the sand. You say that you love Jesus. Do your actions validate that notion? Do you obey him? Jesus presents for us the ultimate litmus test. **If you love Jesus, you will obey Him.** It's that simple.

What about the Orphan though? What does Jesus say about the Orphan? What does the Bible say about the Orphan?

Of sheep and goats

WE'LL examine Matthew 25 for a possible answer. This particular passage occurs during the last week of Jesus' life. He entered Jerusalem triumphantly, riding on a donkey or a colt, depending upon your particular translation. Palm Sunday, the triumphal entry. The people exclaimed, "Hosanna, Hosanna in the highest," literally, God saves.

From this, Jesus went straight to the Temple. I must confess, if I could have been present for any of Jesus' ministry, I would have loved to have witnessed Him in the Temple flipping over the money changers' tables and the tables of those selling doves. "My house will be called a house of prayer, but you are making it a den of thieves!" as He's flipping over tables and basically going berserk. (Matthew 21:13) This is church. This is their house of worship, an assuredly somber place. Yet, Jesus makes this gigantic scene. I try to envision a similar scene today and find I cannot.

Jesus spends the next several days, the concluding days of His life, teaching in and around the Temple and as always, says some pretty profound things and the Pharisees don't like it. The religious leaders don't like it.

They challenge His authority in public a couple of times and predictably, it doesn't go very well for them. They try to trick Jesus a couple of times and corner Him with logic and once again, it doesn't go very well for them as Jesus continues to outwit and humiliate them, publicly. Their frustration mounts with each encounter becoming palpable, building toward the arrest.

On this particular day, though, Jesus is on the Mount of Olives, just east of Jerusalem, and the Apostles come to Him to ask questions. "When will these things happen? What is the sign of Your coming and of the end of the age?" and Jesus teaches them, "wars and rumors of wars" and so forth. Matthew 24 presents some of Jesus' most profound teachings on end times events, depending upon your eschatology, which is not a subject of this work.

He then tells the disciples the parable of the ten virgins followed by the parable of the talents, both teaching Christians to be alert, to be good stewards with what God has entrusted you, because He is coming. Jesus will come, so we must be faithful; we must be ready. Then we get to the passage we will examine in detail.

As we read this passage, let us vow not to read into it. To the best of our ability, let's cast aside whatever preconceptions we may have and read this text at face value. Perhaps we'll ascertain what it is that Jesus is trying to teach us.

When the Son of Man comes in His glory, and all the angels with Him, then He will sit on the throne of His glory. All the nations will be gathered before Him, and He will separate them one from another, just as a shepherd separates the sheep from the goats. He will put the sheep on His right, and the goats on the left. Then the King will say to those on His right, "Come, you who are blessed by My Father, inherit the kingdom prepared for you from the foundation of the world.

*For I was hungry
and you gave Me something to eat;
I was thirsty
and you gave Me something to drink;
I was a stranger and you took Me in;*

I was naked and you clothed Me;
I was sick and you took care of Me;
I was in prison and you visited Me."

Then the righteous will answer Him, "Lord, when did we see You hungry and feed You, or thirsty and give You something to drink? When did we see You a stranger and take You in or without clothes and clothe You? When did we see You sick, or in prison, and visit You?"

And the King will answer them, "I assure you: Whatever you did for one of the least of these brothers of Mine, you did for Me." Then He will also say to those on the left, "Depart from Me, you who are cursed, into the eternal fire prepared for the Devil and his angels!

For I was hungry
and you gave Me nothing to eat;
I was thirsty
and you gave Me nothing to drink;
I was a stranger
and you didn't take Me in;
I was naked
and you didn't clothe Me,
sick and in prison
and you didn't take care of Me."

Then they too will answer, "Lord, when did we see You hungry, or thirsty, or a stranger, or without clothes, or sick, or in prison, and not help You?"

Then He will answer them, "I assure you: Whatever you did not do for one of the least of these, you did not do for Me either."

And they will go away into eternal punishment, but the righteous into eternal life.

Matthew 25:31-46

Did you catch what Jesus is saying here, the gist of this image? Again, let's cast aside your eschatology for a few minutes. Whether there is one judgment at the end or two or three, that concept is not germane to what we are considering with respect to the Orphan. At the end, there will be Judgment. That much, all can pretty much agree upon.

Jesus is saying, at this judgment, *all* of the nations will stand before Him and *all* will be declared as either sheep or goats. Those who took care of the least of these – fed them, clothed them, housed them, visited them in prison and so forth – will be identified as sheep and will inherit the kingdom prepared for them from the foundation of the world.

Those who did not care for the least of these – either didn't feed them, clothe them, house them, take care of them, or visit them in prison – will be identified as goats. To them, Jesus will say, "Depart from Me," and He will cast them into the eternal fire prepared for Satan and his angels where they will receive eternal punishment.

No middle ground exists at this judgment, a sobering thought. Jesus designates all as either a sheep or a goat and He issues surprisingly specific criteria for determining this. Needless to say, one could draw some remarkable, possibly even inaccurate, conclusions from this passage alone.

Blind spots

DAVID Platt, current President of the IMB and former pastor of the Church at Brook Hills in Birmingham, Alabama, wrote an excellent book entitled *Radical*, which I highly recommend. In the book, Platt condemns the status of the church in the west, in America. As one of the youngest pastors of a mega-church, Brook Hills numbers upwards of 10,000 members, Platt had become disillusioned with their prosperity, their wealth.

As evidenced by his selection to the International Mission Board, Platt has served frequently as an overseas missionary, particularly to India, one of the poorer countries in the world and he has seen the need, the poverty. Now, I'm not talking about poverty like not being able to afford a new cell phone. Platt recollects seeing people who have absolutely nothing and it changed him.

In his book, Platt discusses what he calls blind spots.[6] The church in America has blind spots. He cites the historical example of slavery. A mere 200 years ago, all over the country, in and around a thriving and growing church, the nation condoned and supported the selling and owning of human beings as property, slavery. It took a war and thousands of lives sacrificed to end this detestable practice. Consider, though that churchgoers, Christians, likely pastors and deacons and elders all owned slaves. The church, blinded to this, stood idly by. Now, granted that these broad strokes do not include *every* Christian of the day, but they certainly include *many*.

To Platt, a similar condition plagues the western church today concerning poverty. Platt discusses leaving his multi-million dollar church building and seeing his congregation get in their 20-, 30-, 40-thousand dollar vehicles and going home to their several hundred thousand dollar homes and forgetting all about anyone else until next Sunday and all the while, around the world, *people are literally starving to death, every single day,* in Africa, in Asia, in the Middle East, South America. People starve to death while we Americans live in relative lavish luxury.

Even our poor, by comparison, live in relative luxury and for those who become destitute, all forms of safety nets and organizations exist to support and enable someone to get back on their feet. Now, I do not seek to impugn the suffering of our

---

[6] David Platt, *Radical*, (Multnomah Books: Colorado Springs, 2010).

poor. Certainly we have those who suffer, but, collectively speaking, a shameful disparity exists. The western church goes about its daily business largely blind to the suffering of the nations. Will we all be declared as goats at the end?

Now, I agree with Platt, but I do believe another aspect bears mentioning. Certainly America at least prospers far beyond our collective need, but America in general is certainly the most generous country in the world. Pick a natural disaster and see which aid organizations show up from which countries. Haiti, Japan, Indonesia – you'll see Americans and American dollars hard at work. America is a generous country, it's just that our giving, though generous, could certainly be much, much more. How many cars do you need? How many square feet are enough? How many bonus rooms do you need? Do you actually need a bonus room?

Yet, I will submit to you that the western church, the church in America, has an even greater blind spot and perhaps an even more shameful blind spot, a blind spot that exists underneath our collective noses, in our very towns and cities, in our communities, in our figurative back yards. This blind spot is *local.*

Examine the list of criteria Jesus provides in Matthew 25 to distinguish between the sheep and the goats:

feeding the hungry
water for the thirsty
taking in a stranger
clothing the naked
caring for the sick
visiting the imprisoned

Examine this list and consider the commitment. Examine these criteria and consider your personal commitment. Consider commodities of time, resources, money, and most of all, life change or impact. Consider the respective costs.

Of the body

HAVE you ever noticed that Jesus dealt with the physical as well as the spiritual? Mark chapter two tells the story of some men in Capernaum, who bring their paralyzed friend to see Jesus, but the large crowd prevents them from getting in. Undaunted, they climb to the roof somehow bringing their paralyzed friend with them, tear a hole in the ceiling, and lower their friend down to Jesus.

Jesus' response to the man speaks volumes, "Son, your sins are forgiven." (v. 5) Some of the scribes nearby hear this and start debating amongst themselves about Jesus' claim to be able to forgive sins, surely a task reserved for God Himself. Jesus overhears this and heals the paralyzed man. "Pick up your stretcher and go home," He says, simply. Jesus heals the man spiritually, forgiving his sin and then proceeds to heal the man physically.

Jesus dealt with the physical *and* the spiritual frequently. He forgives sin; He casts out demons and He heals people. He feeds people, thousands of people, miraculously. The notion of Jesus neglecting one aspect for the sake of the other borders on ludicrous and would effectively negate the totality of the person of Christ.

Of James and Jesus

PERHAPS no other book of the Bible speaks such contentious truth as the book penned by our Lord's brother,

James. His book was one of the last adopted into the Canon and not without opposition. Martin Luther himself referred to it as an "Epistle of Straw". Yet, the profundity of the truths contained herein do not refute orthodox *Pauline* theology, rather they amplify from a different perspective.

> *What good is it, my brothers, if someone says he has faith, but does not have works? Can his faith save him? If a brother or sister is without clothes and lacks food and one you says to them, "Go in peace, keep warm, and eat well," but you don't give them what the body needs, what good is it? In the same way faith, if it doesn't have works, is dead by itself.*
>
> James 2:15-17

Faith without works is dead! James goes on to say,

> *Show me your faith without works and I will show you faith from my works. You believe that God is one; you do well. The demons also believe, and they shudder.*
>
> James 2:18-19

James contrasted saving faith with a dead faith. Do not misunderstand and miss the point. He goes on to confirm that salvation is through faith by grace alone, yet James confirms the thrust of his argument by asking, if no evidence of your faith exists, do you really have any faith? **If no evidence exists, no indication is given, no work happens as a result of your faith, then do you have a living faith?** James says resolutely, "no", you have a dead faith, a faith that doesn't exist, no faith.

Well, I do plenty of good things? What exactly are you talking about?

James goes on to clarify,

Pure and undefiled religion before our God and Father is this: to look after orphans and widows in their distress and to keep oneself unstained by the world.

James 1:27

Did you catch that? Here is religion, pure religion, undefiled religion. Religion is not a church building. Religion is not a worship service. Religion is not even preaching or listening to preaching. Religion is taking care of orphans and widows. Simple. Keep yourself unstained by the world and take care of orphans and widows. That's religion, pure and undefiled. You want to honor God, take care of orphans and widows. You want to obey God – and we've seen that those who love God, obey Him – take care of orphans and widows.

"Why would James focus on orphans and widows?" a valid question as people suffer all over the world including, but certainly not restricted to, orphans and widows. The answer resides in the intent of the heart. In first century Palestine, orphans and widows represented two of the most helpless classes of society, completely defenseless and destitute, dependent entirely upon someone else to care for them. Not coincidentally, orphans and widows are the least likely to be able to pay someone back or provide a return. They exist in a condition of "distress".

What's the application? What's the hermeneutic here? Today, in western society, widows do not live powerless and helpless as in Jesus' day of first century Palestine. Women today do not live completely dependent upon a man or a family for support, but orphans today, orphans are still orphans, completely dependent upon others and sadly, as is most common, the State. We build institutions and homes and facilities, but none of these will ever replicate the one basic thing that an orphan needs, that an orphan lacks, that of a family.

A Painless Ministry?

LET'S return to Matthew 25. We can and should feed the hungry though we can always do more. Yet, a painless feeding often becomes the order of the day. A drive-by feeding *usually* costs us nothing. You can send clothing or even give clothing in person, but I ask again, what does it cost you? Great prison ministries and great medical missions care for the sick and the imprisoned and address great areas of need, areas that must be addressed, but the one area mentioned by Jesus that bears mentioning and further examination is the notion of taking a stranger, the least of these, into your house, into your home.

This option, this command from Jesus, taking in the homeless, from James, the Orphan, is significant in its inclusiveness. Opening your home to a stranger, specifically an orphan, is no small and insignificant step, never painless, always with a cost. This is major, significant in its reality.

Volunteering at the Red Cross or the Salvation Army, while certainly worthy endeavors, require much, much less of the giver in terms of time, commitment, and even money. Jesus and his brother James are talking about opening our homes, opening our lives to strangers, to orphans, to the least of these, and I can think of fewer *least of these* than the Orphan.

If you have real faith, then it has saved you. Jesus says that real faith is *communicable*, it saves others with real actions, real people meeting real needs. Let your faith resonate in your actions *despite* any cost. You want to have a saving faith? Then have a saving faith, one that saves someone else.

Let's consider my home state of Tennessee. Currently, over 400 orphans reside in state custody, available for immediate adoption. This does not include the hundreds of kids handled by private agencies. Some of these kids reside in shelters, some in facilities, others in foster homes. Now, this certainly seems to be a lot of kids, but I wondered what this number would look like in comparison with the number of families in the state. With a population of roughly 6 million, Tennessee contains approximately 2.5 million households with 2.5 people per household. In light of this, 400 children remain without homes, without a family, available for adoption, immediately. Tennessee contains *millions* of homes while *hundreds* of kids languish without homes. I'll submit that similar conditions exist in other states.

Now, many of these 2.5 million households may not even recognize the issue – one of the reasons I'm felt led to write this book – and many may have already plunged into foster care and adoption. Yet, the statistics are telling in the sheer disparity. Over 700 churches exist in the Nashville area alone, 700 assemblies of God's people in a single city, yet 400 children toil without homes, without families.

Jesus speaks, in Matthew 25, of real faith, saving faith. Again, do not misunderstand. Salvation comes only through faith in and submission to Christ Jesus, repentance and belief. Following regeneration and conversion, we'll begin the process of sanctification, of being set apart and our faith will manifest itself in our attitudes. *Love, joy, peace, patience, kindness, goodness, faithfulness, gentleness, and self control,* the fruit of the Spirit Paul writes about in Galatians 5:22, will permeate our existence. Your faith, *if it is real*, will continually and increasingly guide your actions.

Jesus says that in submission and in salvation, a true saving faith will save others. That means it saves others physically as well as spiritually, just like Jesus did for us and just as He commands and ordains with respect to strangers, widows, and orphans. **An *indicator* of saving faith is that you will care for the *least of these*.** You will feed them, you will clothe them, you will care for them, visit them in prison, and as we discuss here, you will take them into your homes, the least of these, the Orphan.

A Prayerful Paradigm Shift

"**I'LL** pray about it," a bothersome phrase if there ever was one.

We pray and we pray, "Lord bless me, bless my family, bless our existence" and God says, "Look around Church, I *have* blessed you beyond measure."

Still, we pray, "God heal me, Father help me, Father encourage me, Father show me your will" and God says, "I *have*, my child, I have."

Yet we pray, "God lead me, God forgive me," but consider this.

Somewhere, right now, a little boy or a little girl or a young man or a young woman, somewhere they pray a prayer of such simplicity in relation to the grandiose and sometimes hollow, trifling prayers of the average churchgoer. Somewhere a little boy is praying, "God, give me a family." Somewhere a little girl is praying, "God, give me a family."

As a saving faith, God has given us our faith that we might, through it, communicate the love of Christ to the least of these, widows and orphans, by the simplest thing possible, meeting a need and the greatest need of the Orphan is a family.

I've been around foster kids for several years now and one thing has struck me. When asking about where someone has lived, all of them, and I mean all of them, ask, "Where do you stay?"

Where do you stay? Not, where do you live, but where do

you stay, because without a family, kids don't really live. They... stay. Consider Christ's prescription for life. Did He come that they might have a place to stay or a place to actually live?

I have come that they may have life, and that they may have it more abundantly.

John 10:10b

God has equipped you and He has equipped me. God has blessed you and He has blessed me to actually *be* an answer to a prayer for someone else. What if, instead of praying for something for ourselves, be it blessings or protection or guidance, what if we prayed that we might actually become, even embody, an answered prayer in the life of someone else, particularly a kid with no family. James says that this is a living faith. Jesus says it's a saving faith, the type of faith He will recognize at the Judgment.

Yes, but that's your call, not mine. I just can't.

I don't have room.

I have too many of my own kids.

I don't feel led to do this.

I'm just not sure.

Yes, our family has adopted. Ami and I serve as foster parents and have housed numerous children over the years. Yes, the Lord has placed it upon our hearts to open our home to foster kids who age out of the foster system but that doesn't mean I haven't fought it. That doesn't mean I haven't struggled against all of these notions. Believe me when I tell you, I've had all of these thoughts at different times during the journey. I've considered them all.

What if they're dangerous?

What if they're not good kids?

What if they require all of my time to take care of?

I will grant that many of the kids in the system are damaged, damaged like you would not believe. They have been wounded, outcast, abused, neglected, denied, forsaken, betrayed by the very ones who are supposed to love them the most. Yes, but I ask you, *shouldn't these be the ones we lavish love on the most?* Shouldn't these be the ones sought the most? Should we only focus on the "good" ones or should we seek out the ones that we, collectively, as a society and as a Church, that we have cast aside and failed, if nothing else but to hold them tightly and tell them, "We're sorry, it's not your fault"?

I've battled all of these issues and what it always comes back to is… me. I can drive by a homeless guy and throw him a sandwich and it generates minimal impact on me. I can drop of some clothes at Goodwill with minimal impact to me. I can support many different ministries and donate money again, with minimal impact on me. We must support all of these great things, but to open my home, to open my life, there is not a chance that this won't have a life-changing, life-altering, permanent effect upon me, my circumstances, my life. Guess what though, don't you think the child in question could say the same thing? Since when did defending our lifestyle become a hill upon which to die, or a reason to neglect so clear of a call?

Do you have this type of saving faith? I refuse to lie or sugar coat either these truths or the difficulties associated with obedience to these commands, but to those of you who have your own kids, is it ever easy? Do you have a faith that is real, that has real application in the real world, that can have real implications and change the course of a child's life?

Of pure notions

LET'S examine the issue, this command, from an additional angle. As a believer, I am called to imitate my Lord and Savior, Christ Jesus.

By Paul,

Imitate me, as I also imitate Christ...

1 Corinthians 11:1

Make your own attitude that of Christ Jesus...

Philippians 2:5

By John,

The one who says he remains in Him should walk just as He walked... 1 John 2:6

By Jesus,

I give you a new command: Love one another. Just as I have loved you, you must also love one another.

John 13:34

Scripture informs believers that we must love as Jesus loved. We must walk as He walked. We must imitate His attitude. We must imitate Him. Christ sets the example for all that we do and in as much that He has adopted us as sons, how can we not do the same to those who have yet to be adopted?

Consider the notion of true Christ-like love epitomized by the concept of adoption. Christ loves us who offer nothing in return. Christ loves us who are not His children by birthright, but He adopts us into His family with all of the inheritance and rewards inherent in *sonship* and once adopted, we are loved by Him as children of God, as sons.

Consider the physical manifestation of this, the love and adoption of a child not yours by birth. I ask of you, *is there anything more Christ-like than this?* I can think of nothing except perhaps loving my wife in a Christ-like manner, though in all reality, most of us expect and certainly most receive things in return from our wives.

No guarantee of a return exists from the Orphan. In fact, you will likely be called upon to give until you cannot give anymore and then give some more. You may, in fact, never receive except in the knowledge of providing for the most downtrodden of all, the least of these, and fellowship with the Lord in imitating Him. Are you okay with that?

A Desperate Enemy

AS I was preparing to preach a sermon on the Beatitudes of Matthew 5:1-12, it occurred to me that the Bible guarantees persecution for the practicing believer. It occurred to me that if one is not experiencing any kind of persecution it could indicate one of several things. Either you are not being persecuted *yet* or you are just not aware enough to realize in what manner Satan afflicts you. A less desirable consideration is that no one actually knows you are a Christian. You are a *secret* Christian, keeping your faith to yourself and as such, you pose no threat to the Prince of this World and he does not target you for persecution. The Bible certainly knows nothing of such a Christian.

Persecution often serves as an indicator of spiritual effectiveness. Does the frantic assault upon the sanctity of marriage surprise anyone? Does the world's devaluing of sexual purity and the nuclear family surprise anyone? Does the multi-generational assault upon the veracity and inerrancy of Scripture surprise anyone? Consider that the Enemy even assails the institution of adoption.

One of the most effective strategies in defeating any enemy is assimilation. Think of Alexander the Great and the idea of Hellenism. The Greeks conquered and subdued a vast swath of the planet by forcibly assimilating conquered populations into their own culture – religion, politics, social constructs. This effectively established a solid base of support requiring much less oversight from the military providing them much greater freedom of maneuver to continue the conquest without fretting about a bothersome occupation.

Let's stretch it out a little further. Consider the rapper Ice Cube if you will. Ice Cube was born out of the early 90's rap group NWA – you can research the acronym on your own. NWA was anti-establishment, anti-police, anti-white. They were one of the first gangster rap groups and they rapped with a vulgar ferocity, a stridency of purpose.

Yet, something curious began to happen. As the group and then Ice Cube became more and more successful, their audience slowly changed from all black to mixed to almost all white. Before long, white teenage boys packed NWA shows as the group broke up and the artists went their separate ways.

Ice Cube launched a successful solo career and got into movies and as the world *which he previously decried* showered him with more and more money, the stridency of his message faded until he became a caricature of his former angry, cop-hating self. As a final coup-de-grâce, he is slated to star in the most recent addition of the Teenage Mutant Ninja Turtles movie next year. Somewhere I hear EAZY-E rolling over in his grave. The point though, is that assimilation is decidedly effective in dulling the sharpness of an idea or even an ideology.

Consider marriage. As the God-ordained building block of society and perfect image of the relationship between Christ and the Church, Satan absolutely hates marriage, hates everything that it stands for. The world has launched an all-out assault on the actual institution of marriage in a number of different ways but perhaps even more effectively, has begun to co-opt the institution, infiltrating the concept with ideas that are the antithesis of biblical marriage.

Unbiblical unions, pre-nuptial agreements, divorce on demand and many other perversions dilute the sanctity and witness of holy matrimony. Nowadays, you must even clarify exactly what you are talking about when you mention the idea of marriage.

All of this to say that the Enemy must loathe the institution of adoption and not surprisingly, the institution is under an increasingly effective assault. The very fact that we require adoption agencies and state organizations to fill the void where the Church has failed serves as a testament to the subtle effectiveness of the Enemy. The sheer volume of bureaucratic red-tape one must wade through for one's family to be considered for foster care or adoption is mind-boggling.

The expenses can run rampant. Hidden fees, attorney fees, court costs, agency fees – all of these can drive the price of adoption into the tens of thousands of dollars. The certification process itself is daunting, intrusive and time consuming and our courts are every bit as inefficient as you've heard. Many caseworkers are overworked and underpaid and many of the cases drag out for years. Is it any wonder that some folks shy away?

As secular agencies begin to dominate the institution and the world via secular governments has redefined the nuclear family, orphans increasingly find themselves adopted into anything but traditional families. The Church has not only ceded the institution to the state and secular organizations but has ceded the very actuality of the concept. Increasingly, an orphan might find himself adopted into a decidedly ungodly union.

Well what's wrong with that?

At least the child has a home.

I do not intend to exegete the anti-biblical concept of pragmatism but suffice it to say that choosing between less than biblical notions is not within the revealed will of the Lord our God. One might as well say, "Well, I don't cheat on my wife, I just consume pornography. She doesn't know about it and at least we're happy."

Yet this assault reminds us, in reflection, of the absolute importance of adoption. Adoption is critical. Adoption is life or death. As Satan knows better than any one of us, adoption is a Gospel issue. Is it any wonder the Enemy determinedly chips away at this vehicle of God's holy and perfect will?

Last Things – Greatest Things

MY pursuit is Christ. My passion is Christ. Just to be clear, all other zealotry springs forth from Christ, as He abides. I seek to know Him. Paul says it best,

> *But as for me, I will never boast about anything except the cross of our Lord Jesus Christ.*
>
> Galatians 6:14

In desperation, we seek Him. We call out for Him. We pursue Him. We've examined the functional aspect of His abiding and the logical conclusions concerning adoption, but I'd like to return to ontology, an examination of His actual being. Allow me to regress from what He actually does to who He actually is, His very nature. May we yet discover a catalyst.

As we seek to behold Him who is worthy, Jesus, I remind you that *He* is found in the Orphan. He is the Orphan. If you seek after Jesus, you will find Him in the Orphan. As you minister to the Orphan, you minister to Jesus Himself. As you care for the Orphan, you care for Jesus Himself.

In the broken dreams of helpless children, Jesus is found. In the quiet suffering of the Orphan, Jesus resides. Jesus exists as the longing in each child's heart for the love of a father, the love of a mother. Returning to the *protoevangelium*, never forget that ultimately, it is the heal of Jesus that Satan ultimately bruised and indeed, still bruises this very day.

Though the functional aspect speaks clearly to the primacy of adoption it is this return to the personhood of Jesus that solidifies our conclusions. **If you seek to behold the face of Christ, gaze no further than the face of the nearest orphan.** Peer deeply into his eyes and see the eyes of the man of suffering who knew what sickness was. See a man despised and rejected, a man that people turned away from, a man unvalued, a man stricken and afflicted. Drink deeply of his pain. Revel in his abandonment. When you behold the Orphan, you behold Christ. Let us go to Him. There is *No Higher Call*!

But you know these things. You know these things. The Holy Spirit is revealing this to you. The question resides in your will and the issue of subordination, convenience. At some point, acknowledgement must prompt obedience.

I recall one night, several years ago, as I sat holding my young adopted son in my arms late at night. As a crack, cocaine, fetal alcohol syndrome baby, he rarely slept for more than two hours at a time. This one particular night, I sat holding him while he raged as my exhausted wife desperately sought a few hours of sleep. I wept quietly, begging him to go to sleep, praying that God would heal him of these demons that tormented him and I would not trade that night with him or any of the others for the world.

My reward is in the quiet and confident trust my son has in me, his father. My reward is in the unadulterated affection of all my sons, who've adopted me as their father.

Brothers and sisters, acknowledge God's call concerning the Orphan. Cast aside your fear. Cling no more to your lifestyle, concern over your quality of life. Submit and eternally impact the life of another, a young child. This highest of calls is clear and simple, leaving one troubling question, a question that lingers quite irritably.

Will you obey?

> See then that you walk circumspectly,
> not as fools but as wise,
> redeeming the time,
> because the days are evil.
>
> Ephesians 5:15-16 (NKJV)

QUESTIONS

1. Consider Bonhoeffer's statement, *"Costly grace is the gospel which must be sought again and again... what has cost God much cannot be cheap for us."* What does he mean by this? How have you seen this idea manifest itself in your life? The life of the church? Have you seen "cheap" grace in action?

2. Read James 1:27.

    a. Why does James single out widows and orphans.

    b. Consider your local church. How does the idea of this passage manifest itself in ministry?

    c. Do you agree with the exegetical bridge of orphans from James 1:27 to "the least of these" from Matthew 25:31-46? Why or why not? What is the logical application of this?

3. Consider the phrase, "I'll pray about it." How is this phrase abused? Have you witnessed this? Have you abused this phrase?

4. Consider the call and biblical command to imitate Jesus. How does this resonate with respect to the notion of orphans and adoption?

5. This work claims that, "at some point, acknowledgement must prompt obedience." What are the implications of this phrase?

6. In light of this chapter, discuss/consider the Bible's call to physical adoption. In general, what is the Bible's stance on adoption?

7. Has what you have read influenced your views at all? How has the Holy Spirit spoken to you?

> having predestined us to adoption as sons by Jesus Christ to Himself, according to the good pleasure of His will,
>
> Ephesians 1:5 (NKJV)

Chapter 5

I'VE wondered how many live blinded to the fight, blinded to the struggle, blinded to the fact that children live and die in destitution right under our collective noses, perishing under the crushing weight of neglect. I've wondered how many live *willingly* blinded, turning a blind eye to that which is obvious.

Right now, as you read this, a believer agonizes over living his best life now, how to live life to the fullest and receive the entire measure of God's blessing. Right now, a child wonders where his next meal will come from and whether a family will ever love him. These are facts, sad but indisputable. The cry of the Orphan is the shame of the Church.

The cry of the Orphan is the shame of the Church.

One need not look too deeply into Scripture to be confronted with the reality of numerous stark truths. As the issue of the Orphan rouses my passions, I've struggled with this chapter much more so than the others as I desperately don't want to infer ideas from Scripture that Scripture does not contain. I desperately desire to remain within the bounds of orthodoxy, and I know that the Gospel offends enough on its own without me wielding it in an offensive manner. Yet, only with great difficulty could one deny these rather obvious needs and commands, the natural result of which inevitably force some striking conclusions.

If Scripture does not provoke a certain measure of discomfort, indeed, increasing discomfort, then perhaps one is not reading it correctly. As James points out,

But be doers of the Word and not hearers only, deceiving ourselves. Because if anyone is a hearer of the word and not a doer, he is like a man looking at his own face in a mirror. For he looks at himself, goes away, and immediately forgets what kind of man he was.

James 1:22-24

When we, the Church, view our collective lives through the lens of Scripture, certain undeniable truths become apparent. Sometimes these truths are quite painful to consider for even a moment. Scripture is as a mirror, revealing that which lies hidden in the depths of our hearts, all of the sordid remnants of the Old Man vying in the darkness for a grasp upon our will, the very engine of our actions.

The mirror of Scripture illuminates that which we'd likely rather leave in the shadows and as long as these things remain obscured from Illumination, the cry of the Orphan will continue to fall upon deaf ears.

The Little African Girl

MY oldest daughter, the rebel, asked me a difficult question once, one that many Christians struggle to answer, "What about the little girl in Africa?"

What about the little girl in Africa who's never heard about Jesus? Will she be condemned? If so, doesn't this speak to a distinct level of unfairness on behalf of God? If not, then doesn't that deny the clear testimony of Jesus and exclusivity from say, John 14:6, "No one comes to the Father except through me"? For many, this question poses a rather marked conundrum.

So my eldest, my rebel, posed this question with a certain smugness, convinced that the efficacy of her logic would render me speechless, not so that she might undermine aspects of our shared faith but rather that she might, no doubt, cast doubt upon the veracity of *any* claims I might make, specifically more sensitive ones concerning boys and privileges and the like, both somewhat contentious topics at the time.

I must admit that my first response rang hollow. Nowadays, I can speak much more assuredly on the issue. I can see the worldview paradigm shift that must occur to address this issue for what it is, a proper understanding of the nature of the supposed 'innocence' of any man reconciled with a proper understanding of the sovereignty of God. Back then, though, I didn't have the juice. At the time, I meekly responded with something concerning the perfect justice of God and retreated to my bedroom, leaving my daughter to gloat.

Sulking in my bedroom, I complained to my lovely wife who was reading the Bible while enjoying a most puzzling activity – to a man anyway – a bubble bath. Looking over her shoulder, I read the following passage:

The word of the LORD came to me: "Son of man, speak to your people and tell them: Suppose I bring the sword against a land, and the people of that land select a man from among them, appointing him as their watchman, and he sees the sword coming against the land and blows his trumpet to warn the people. Then, if anyone hears the sound of the trumpet but ignores the warning, and the sword comes and takes him away, his blood will be on his own head. Since he heard the sound of the trumpet but ignored the warning, his blood is on his own hands. If he had taken warning, he would have saved his life.

However, if the watchman sees the sword coming but doesn't blow the trumpet, so that the people aren't warned, and the sword comes and takes away their lives, then they have been taken away because of their iniquity, but I will hold the watchman accountable for their blood.

Ezekiel 33:1-6

Ha! This was it! The good Lord had provided. I stormed back down the hallway and barged into my daughter's room trumpeting things about Ezekiel and the watchman and personal responsibility to share the Gospel, how the result is not up to us, how we are the watchman and so we should focus upon our actions and leave judgment up to God! Thus, our job is to sound the trumpet to all who may hear it, including the little girl in Africa, and if we don't, then her blood is upon our hands. Yes! Victory in Jesus!

Now, I'll be the first to acknowledge that my understanding lacked some specific nuances, but hey, it was enough to allow me to declare temporary victory over my daughter, the rebel! Yet, as I reflected upon the Orphan, another more sobering application of this particular passage came to mind concerning this work.

The Watchman and the Gospel

AS you hopefully saw from Chapter 2, the issue of the Orphan is very clearly a Gospel issue. From the pages of Scripture, the Orphan cries out for a family, for a home, for love. Yet, most stridently, the Orphan calls out, like all of those separated from Christ, the Orphan calls out for something unspoken, something unspeakable to them, something to fill a certain unfillable void.

The cry of the Orphan colludes with the collective wail of the entirety of the Unregenerate who groan under the weight of their sin, yearning for the unknowable, suffering a sickness only cured by the Gospel, Christ and Him crucified. **Will you be the one to carry the Message?** Will you sound the trumpet as the faithful watchman?

I pray that through this work, you've seen the truth of the need, the truth of the call and now, unfortunately, you have no choice but to stand as the watchman to which Ezekiel speaks. Sin destines all of those separated from Christ for judgment, for the sword. Now, you have been equipped with the knowledge of a great need, a great harvest, right in your very town, in your very community. You know that the sword comes. You know about it. Will you sound the trumpet or will the Lord one day hold you accountable for the blood of the Orphan?

Scripture tells us that all men will give an account some day, *on that day*.

So then, each of us will give an account of himself to God.

Romans 14:12

I confess that I envision this day with no small measure of dread. To be clear, God has forgiven my sins through the blood of the Lamb, Christ Jesus, and He has imputed His righteousness to me. When God looks upon me, He sees and will see the righteousness found only in the Son. Yet I will still give an account. In some way, I will account for my words, my actions, or in this case, my lack thereof. As such, how could we ever explain away the blood of the Orphan?

The sound of the guns...

INTERESTINGLY, as our church began to preach through this issue and encourage and exhort the body to get involved, some resisted. Many passively resisted, refusing to attend church events that highlighted the issue, quietly ignoring the topic. A few actively resisted, to my eternal surprise, actually speaking out *against* adoption.

Adoption is dangerous.

I'd never subject my family to that.

They belong with their own parents.

(Even to my astonishment) Adoption is evil!

Granted, I tend to militarize most subjects. Twenty years of service and four years of military college will do that to a man. Yet, the Army has a tendency to simplify things to the greatest extent possible which is a very useful quality to a man of limited capacity such as myself. The fog of battle and friction of warfare necessitates this. When bullets fly and confusion runs rampant, this is not the time to consider and ponder complex thoughts. A Colonel I used to know would frequently exhort us cadets, "In the absence of further orders... attack!" usually punctuated by a hearty and guttural, "Hooah!"

Saying it in a different manner, there are those who run toward the sound of the guns versus those who do not. When gun play breaks out, some seek out the fight, running to engage, while others tremble meekly behind cover, praying for their own safety, never minding their mission, their duty, or their comrades in peril.

Conceptually, Jesus would encourage us, with respect to the Orphan, to run toward the sound of the proverbial guns. They thunder relentlessly. At a banquet at Matthew's (Levi's) home, Jesus dined with sinners and other tax collectors. The Pharisees and the scribes took exception and asked, "Why do you eat and drink with tax collectors and sinners?" (Luke 5:30) to which Jesus replied,

> *The healthy don't need a doctor, but the sick do. I have not come to call the righteous, but sinners to repentance.*
>
> Luke 5:31

Jesus always ran toward the sound of the guns. He went where the greatest need was. He dined with sinners and tax collectors. He brought the cure to the sick, forsaking the healthy. He understood where the greatest need, the greatest fight was. He ran to the sound of the guns. Further, back to James,

> *So it is a sin for the person who knows to do what is good and doesn't do it.*
>
> James 4:17

James reminds us that, when we know what to do, when we know what is good, and we don't do it, we are, in effect, sinning. Other than some specifically mentioned sins such as sexual sin, all sin is equally damning in the eyes of the Father. **No degrees of sin exist.**

When we hear the distant roar of the battle and meekly and *safely* cower in the thicket, we sin. When we lounge in the comfortable presence of the healthy and forsake the poor, the downtrodden, the spiritually bankrupt, the dispossessed, the lost, we sin.

Jesus calls the believer, the true believer, to action.

A Call to Greatness

EACH year in this country, just over 100,000 foster children become eligible for adoption meaning that a judge has terminated parental rights or the parents have willingly surrendered their rights.

How many believers are there who could adopt? I know that there are approximately 16 million Southern Baptists in the more than 42,000 Southern Baptist churches nationwide, meaning that there are roughly 138 Southern Baptists for each child in the system, waiting for adoption. What of the Methodists, Catholics, Lutherans, Bible Congregations, Pentecostals, Episcopalians, Presbyterians, Assemblies, non-denominational congregations, et. al.?

It gets worse. A 2013 Barna Group study revealed that 5% of professing Christians have adopted which is only slightly better than the rate for the general population of 2% for non-believing adults. Just 5% is all who feel and respond to the weight of this conviction, who yield to the Call. The study further revealed that just 3% of Christians have served as foster parents. In comparison, 38% of Christians have "considered" adoption and 31% have "considered" fostering.[7]

I'll say it again. The cry of the Orphan is the shame of the Church.

Yet, a chance for greatness resides in the Call.

The opportunity for triumph abounds!

As a friend of mine, a pastor, negotiated the extensive certification process to become a foster family, he asked me a question. They already had 3 girls of their own and if they got a

---

[7] Barna Group, "Five Things You Need to Know About Adoption," accessed December 2014,
(https://www.barna.org/barna-update/family-kids/643-5-things-you-need-to-know-about-adoption).

girl, she would have to share a bedroom with at least two other girls. Should they agree to take a girl, he wanted to know, based upon potentially cramped housing conditions?

As we spoke, I asked him that if you fast-forwarded 20 years, do you think a foster girl would look back and regret having a family, even if it meant she had to share a room with one or more other kids. Would she really be saying, "you know, I wish I'd have just stayed in the foster system and had my own room"?

The answer is obvious. A few weeks later, my friend got his first foster child, a girl, and it is highly likely based on the circumstances that they will adopt her. She will be his daughter... and will have to share a bedroom with her two sisters. What a glorious testimony. A child who had no home, now has a loving father and mother...forever. Her life has been irreversibly changed in a manner that she'll never comprehend.

As Isaiah declares triumphantly,

Enlarge the site of your tent,
and let your tent curtains be stretched out;
do not hold back;
lengthen your ropes,
and drive your pegs deep.

Isaiah 54:2

God calls us to enlarge our tents, to stretch out the canvas, to lengthen our ropes, driving our pegs deep. As the fields are white for the harvest, Scripture resolutely declares, harvest first your own fields and if you have done so, then seek to add to your harvest by adding to your own fields. Though I may be called upon to harvest another person's field, I have certainly been called upon to harvest my own fields and to expand the number of fields that I have for the harvest.

Yes, the cry of the Orphan is the shame of the Church.

Yet, the Orphan is the glorious realization of where to find Christ!

The Orphan provides an opportunity for us, believers, to truly act as Christ, to conform to His image, to engage as He did, to adopt as He adopts, to love as He loves. As Carey preached, "Expect great things from God; attempt great things for God."

The movie *10,000 B.C.* aptly describes the greatness of this endeavor as one man explains to a boy why his father was not around during his childhood. He had gone to literally save the world.

- A good man draws a circle around himself and cares for those within. His woman, his children.

- Other men draw a larger circle and bring within their brothers and sisters.

- But some men have a great destiny. They must draw around themselves a circle that includes many, many more.

- Your father was one of those men. You must decide whether you are, as well.

Enlarge your tent, O Believer. Stretch out your ropes. Drive your tent pegs deep. A vast multitude languishes without shelter. The sorry fact is that many Christians will die never having stepped out on behalf of the Lord. Many Christians will come face to face with the glorified Christ having missed that to which they were called.

What a glorious testimony before Christ our Lord if you were to approach Him with a full quiver, a tent stretched to capacity, tent pegs literally bending from the strain of the stretched out ropes. "Jesus, I did what I could, what you called me to do", our quiet, humble, yet glorious testimony before Him. "Well done, good and faithful servant."

What if a child, a young man or a young woman, could say

that their father and mother chose to love them. They didn't have to, but they did. They heeded the Call. I can think of nothing higher.

> And because you are sons, God has sent forth the Spirit of His Son into your hearts, crying out, "Abba, Father!"
>
> Galatians 4:6 (NKJV)

Bradford Smith

Chapter Five Discussion Questions

QUESTIONS

1. This work makes the claim that, "the cry of the orphan is the shame of the church." Do you agree with this statement? What are the implications of this statement?

2. Read Romans 14:12.

   a. Coupled with the exposition on Ezekiel 33, what are the implications of this passage?

   b. Does this thought resonate in your daily life? Why or why not?

   c. What would happen if more Christians lived in view of this passage?

3. Under the heading "Last Things" this work discusses statistics concerning Christians and adoption.

   a. What are your thoughts on these statistics?

   b. Does it say anything that Christians and non-Christians adopt at a similar rate?

   c. Is there anything else that stands out about the statistics in this section?

4. Read James 4:17.

   a. What does James mean by this passage?

   b. Have you sinned in this way? If you are willing, discuss with the group a specific time you may have sinned in this way.

5. Has this chapter spoken to you in any way? Is the Orphan your responsibility?

> He has shown you, O man, what *is* good;
> And what does the Lord require of you
> But to do justly, To love mercy,
> And to walk humbly with your God?
>
> Micah 6:8 (NKJV)

CHAPTER 6

I'D like to examine another aspect of this issue, an aspect that may actually hit closer to home and in all reality, requires a much more thorough look than this work will permit. Yet, a cursory examination proves necessary, useful even.

I'll start with a question. Are you a father, as in, do you have a biological child? Are you engaged, active, present? Now, as a father myself, these questions resonate personally, but Scripture and the reality of our existence demonstrates the importance of the answers to these questions, the sheer *vitality*.

Let's examine the Word of God.

*Sing to God! Sing praises
to His name.*

*Exalt Him who rides
on the clouds -*

*His name is Yahweh -
and rejoice before Him.*

*A father of the fatherless
and a champion of widows
is God in His holy dwelling.*

*God provides homes for those
who are deserted.*

He leads prisoners
to prosperity,
but the rebellious live
in a scorched land.

Psalm 68:4-6

David, the psalmist proclaims God's majesty. Previously, he pronounces judgment upon God's enemies (v. 1-3) and then issues this series of imperatives. Sing! Exalt! Rejoice! He is Yahweh, the self-existence One, the Creator, the LORD. He is "father of the fatherless" and a "champion of widows". (v. 5) It is significant that David, after exhorting the reader to sing, exalt, and rejoice, first describes God in this particular fashion, a father to the fatherless and a champion of the widow, the very essence of God.

David then proceeds to describe what God does. He "provides homes for those who are deserted" and "leads prisoners to prosperity." God actively addresses the physical and spiritual needs of the downtrodden, the destitute.

The Affliction of Young Men

INTERESTINGLY, the Hebrew word for orphan, *yathowm*, is almost always translated as "fatherless". As we've spoken to the orphan in the traditional sense of the word, the fatherless cannot be denied, must not be ignored. Though not technically orphans as we would define them, the fatherless demand attention. As we'll see, a modern application of the Old Testament treatment regarding the fatherless is entirely appropriate.

To this point, we've defined the spiritual battlefield, the

realm of the actual life and death struggle that takes place around us every single day. Let's clarify roles a bit.

God has ordained the man as the leader of the home and the leader of the church and when I say leader, I am speaking in a spiritual perspective. Whether you like it or not, agree with it or not, this is the case. Yet, man has abdicated his responsibility in an increasingly significant way, ceding leadership in the home and the church to whomever may actually fill the void, frequently women.

Make no mistake about it and despite what many may claim, this is to the detriment of the nation and the Church. God's revealed will knows nothing of a man lacking this responsibility, this requirement to lead.

As the war rages, it rages fiercely against the young men of the west, the young men of this nation, consuming many of them. The conflict afflicts young women certainly, but more as a natural outflow of the affliction of young men.

The Bible defines godly expectations for young men. Return to the Garden, if you will. Young men are to commune with God, work, marry, have children and bring them up in the ways of the Lord. Young men are to love their wives as Christ loves the church, making her holy, washing her in the water that is the Word of God. Yet, the world absolutely floods young men with the overtly ungodly.

For as he thinks within himself, so he is.

Psalm 23:7

"Garbage in - garbage out" is the biblical notion. Consider the tidal wave of confusing messages that floods young men today. Biblical illiteracy plagues our nation as literally, second generation un-churched parents raise their children with absolutely no consideration for the teachings of the Bible. With respect to work, an increasingly prevalent entitlement mentality pervades the thought patterns of young men and many only know a father who has exhibited this very thing along with a healthy dose of irresponsibility.

Sexual issues plague young men as they languish in confusion over even the most basic and critical aspects of a relationship between a man and woman. Pornography stains the collective conscience of a generation of young men. The music he listens to reinforces every stereotype and he is surrounded by young women who confirm all of the poisonous untruths he's learned about the fairer sex. Rampant substance abuse further exacerbates these issues.

Is it any wonder that young men are failing at life, are failing at even the most basic aspects of being a productive member of society, are failing at being a man, which begs the obvious question, *where are the fathers?!*

Where are the fathers?

Because this is a war, because the enemy desperately lays siege to an absolutely critical institution, the institution of manhood, young men desperately need a champion, a protector, a defender, a judge. Young men need a father.

Modern Man

CONSIDER the caricature of manhood that modernity embraces. In short, modern man is a doofus, a fool, an oaf. Balance this image with biblical exhortations concerning wisdom and foolishness. The entire book of Proverbs contrasts the wise man and the fool. Consider these excerpts from Ecclesiastes chapter 10:

*Even when the fool walks along the road, his
heart lack sense...
The lips of a fool consume him...
The struggles of fools weary them...
Because of laziness, the roof caves in, because
of negligent hands the house leaks...*

The author seems to perfectly capture the modern depiction of manhood. Perhaps no contemporary platform better characterized this depiction than *The Man Show* which aired from 1999 to 2004. *The Man Show* focused on the things that men enjoy, beer and women, what else. Frequently depicting scantily clad women bouncing on trampolines, it normally concluded with the hosts and the audience chugging a mug of beer. Humorous though this may be, a generation of young men has bought into this notion of manhood.

I had a conversation once with a young man in our care who was walking out on his girlfriend and their young son, leaving town. As I exhorted him to assume responsibility, to stay, to be the father his son so desperately needs, he responded, "This is what a man does!" in exasperation. He truly believes this and why shouldn't he? This is what he's been taught. His father had walked out on him when he was just a baby.

Society demonizes manhood today, authentic manhood. Errant and misplaced feminism encourages boys to act like girls. Schools and parents squash even the slightest hint of aggression or competitiveness. My little nephew's school actually suspended him for pointing his fingers at another little boy like a gun, a timeless gesture utilized by little boys lacking an actual toy gun since the dawn of man.

In fact, who is the ideal man today? It is the homosexual man. Consider media depictions of the gay man versus the previously discussed depictions of the straight man as an oaf and a fool. The homosexual man is always the best looking, the best dressed, the politest, the funniest...*always*.

Yet, despite these modern perversions, the Bible practically brims with masculinity and exhortations to masculinity.

Be watchful, stand firm, act like men...

1 Corinthians 16:13

When I was a child, I spoke like a child, I
thought like a child, I reasoned like a child.
When I became a man, I put aside childish things.

1 Corinthians 13:11

Strength. Courage. God calls men to well, act like men, and here is the crux of the matter at hand. Manhood is inherently tied to fatherhood. Manhood is an essential component of fatherhood and how are young men supposed to learn about manhood? From their father! God has ordained fathers as the primary instructors on authentic manhood for young men.

In fact, in this war, in this battle, no greater weapon exists than godly men wielding the sword of the spirit that is the Word of God, leading and teaching their sons, serving as fathers, champions.

An Ugly Reality

STATISTICS bear this out. In the United States, approximately one in three children (24 million) live without a biological father. Of those, 20 million live with mothers only, absent even a step-father. Consider this:

- Father-child contact is associated with increased socio-economic functioning, fewer behavioral problems, and higher academic achievement.

- Fatherless children are four times as likely to live in poverty. In 2011, 12 percent of children of married couples lived in poverty. Nearly 45 percent of those living with single mothers lived in poverty.

- Infant mortality rates are double for unmarried mothers.

- Fatherless children experience higher rates of incarceration, teen pregnancy, future child abuse, obesity, emotional and mental issues.

- 63% of youth suicides come from fatherless homes (5 times the average).

- 90% of homeless and runaway children come from fatherless homes (9 times the average).

- 71% of high school drop-outs come from fatherless homes (9 times the average).

- 85% of youths in prison come from fatherless homes.[8]

Even secular studies acknowledge that a father's love and presence is a vital factor in predicting social, emotional, and cognitive development and functioning of children and young adults.

Even more than that, the child is likely to imitate the faith of the father, or lack thereof. The father sets the spiritual tone for the family. The studies all say the same things. If both parents regularly attend church, the children have a good chance of growing up to be regular church attenders. If the father does not attend regularly, almost certainly the children will not become regular church attenders. Interestingly, if the father is a regular

---

[8] National Fatherhood Initiative, accessed December 2014, (http://www.fatherhood.org/bid/190202/The-Father-Absence-Crisis-in-America-Infographic).

attender and the mother is not, the chances that the children will become regular attenders actually increases from when both parents are regular attenders.

The statistics for absentee fathers speak just as clearly. The children of absentee fathers almost always do not become regular church attenders, no matter the faith habits of the mother. Equally as interesting, if the father is absent due to death, the children possess a high chance of becoming regular church attenders almost as if the children know and understand and forgive his absence. However, it is clear. The father sets the spiritual tone for the family, either positive or negative.

Engagement, an Obvious Conclusion

AS such, I can think of three obvious conclusions that resonate from this information as this works seeks to answer that most critical of questions, "What does God want me to do?"

First, I won't revisit the previous body of this work to exhort you to adopt. Consider adoption. Support adoption. I can think of nothing that embodies the sheer masculine nature of our Lord and Father more than to take in another and to love them as your own, bringing them up in the ways of God.

Second, and slightly less obvious, but father your children, your sons. I'll ask again. Do you have children? Are you active, present, engaged? Act like men, engage. Act like men, be present. Act like men, father your children; raise your sons. Sons in particular languish desperate for godly fathers. They *thirst*.

Act like men and raise your sons. I'll resist the urge to address divorce, but act like men and stay. If things absolutely do not work out between you and the mother of your sons, then stay anyway. Raise your sons. Consider their thirst over your own selfish desires.

Let's digress temporarily. What if we acted like men and reserved our sexual energy for the wife of our youth? How many of these issues might actually never become issues? Yet, that would require an even further subordination of our own fleshly desires and since the world would consider that non-sequitur, then I guess we'll move on.

The final conclusion we'll consider concerns fathers in general, not necessarily our own father, but fathers. I'm speaking of the unified body of godly men, fathers, who imitate God in their collective shepherding of a nation's young men. Since millions of young men, who do not and will not have a father, already populate this nation, we must consider this present reality.

Fathers and Champions

I'VE had many fathers: my high school football coach, my best friend's dad, Mr. McBride (yes, the same one from chapter one), my first commanding officer.

In many ways, the military has always embodied this notion. The military has provided, through the years, a council of strong godly fathers for a generation of wayward young men. Can't find your way in society, join the military. They'll set you straight, and how, with strong male leadership. This notion is even more deeply ingrained in church polity. God ordains a plurality of elders - strong, Christian men - to lead the local body of believers, the church.

Men invented the concept of professional clergy, the idea of laymen, and a separation between them and the common Christian. God conscripted elders to shepherd, teach, and protect the flock. This is no accident. He knows that no greater weapon exists than a unified body of godly men wielding the sword of the spirit that is the Word of God...acting like men.

O' man, may I entreat you to examine yourself? Test yourself.

Older men are to be self-controlled, worthy of respect, sensible, and sound in faith, love, and endurance. Likewise, encourage young men to be sensible about everything. Set an example of good works yourself, with integrity and dignity in your teaching.

Titus 2:2,6-7

Paul assumes that older men will teach the younger men how to act. How do you measure against this biblical standard? How is your self-control? Are you worthy of respect? Sensible? Sound in faith, love, and endurance?

I entreat you, O' man, get serious about life. Get off the couch. Quit wasting your life in things that do not matter, playing video games, pursuing the instant gratification of the flesh. Be strong. Be courageous. Act like men.

How can you teach your own sons, this nation's sons, if you still act like a boy yourself?

The Bible speaks consistently to this notion of a godly council of fathers shepherding a nation's youth.

Iron sharpens iron, and one man sharpens another.

Proverbs 27:17

One generation will declare Your works to the next and will proclaim your mighty acts.

Psalm 145:4

Even when I am old and gray, God, do not abandon me. Then I will proclaim Your power to another generation, Your strength to all who are to come.

Psalm 71:18

Back to Psalm 68. Do you imitate God? Are you a father to the fatherless? A champion to the widow? Everywhere, young men are dying of thirst, thirsty for the love and leadership of a godly father. This is truly an epidemic of biblical proportions, the dearth of fathers in western society, and God is calling you to act like a man, to be a father to your own sons, a father to the fatherless.

Decide in your heart to get involved. Open your eyes and look around. You won't have to look far. The fatherless are *everywhere*, literally.

What if, when a young man treated a young woman in a certain way, a unified council of godly fathers was present to confront the young man and collectively declare, "No son, that's not how we treat our women."

What if, when a young man defiantly declared his right to receive things, a unified council of godly fathers was on hand to say, "No son, we work for things around here."

What if, when a young man spits in the face of God, triumphantly declaring his independence from the Creator, a group of fathers, godly men who lived out the biblical model of manhood, was on hand to say, "No son, that's not the way. This is the way. Let me show you."

I've seen all of this first-hand as the fatherless have frequently occupied my residence. I've seen the devastating and *predictable* impact of fathers who have abandoned their children, their sons. But I've seen the converse as well. I've seen the hope, the power manifest in godly men, fathers, collectively stewarding young men.

One of the fatherless in my home had an issue in social studies. He hated his teacher and hated social studies as well and as such, his grades got continually worse and then we got a phone call concerning disrespect toward his teacher. I reprimanded him, exhorted him, but I could tell by the distant look in his eyes that my rebuke was falling short.

Yet, when we went to see his baseball coach, a strong, godly man, things began to change. As his baseball coach and I discussed his transgressions with him present, I could see his demeanor begin to change. His coach suggested that, if things didn't change immediately, then he could sit out the next game after explaining to his teammates why he let them down and further, he would not only sit out, he would have to watch from the bench. He got the point, and things began to change for the better. We didn't really have issues with social studies after this.

Yet, here was the power of the Father displayed in the unified council of godly men shepherding the fatherless, investing in them, immersing themselves in their lives. They exist, by the millions. What will you do?

So we return to our original exhortation. Do you father your own children? Are you present, active, engaged? Will you father another, lengthening the ropes of your tent? Will you father the fatherless, investing in the legion of *yathowm* that populate your very city?

As you consider what it is that God is calling you to do, I pray that you'd consider that perhaps it is much simpler than you'd ever imagine. Perhaps God is calling you to simply be a father, to father the fatherless. The simplicity of this call is exceeded only be the potential, the power.

I can think of *No Higher Call*.

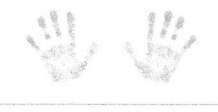

Bradford Smith

Chapter Six Discussion Questions

QUESTIONS

1. Review Genesis 2:18 and 1 Timothy 2:12,13. What do these verses explicitly and implicitly say about the relationships and roles of men and women? Complementarianism is the view that males and females complement each other in their different roles and duties. What are your views on this? How do you reconcile this with equality or a seeming inequality in the male/female roles? How do you see this idea manifest in the church? the home?

2. Do you personally know fatherless children or are you fatherless yourself? Compare and contrast the reality you've observed of the fatherless versus those who were raised in a traditional home with a mother and a father. Why are fatherless children becoming more prevalent? Why are there many more fatherless than motherless children? Does this relate to your answers in question 1? Does this relate to the Fall described in Genesis 3?

3. This chapter makes the claim that the spiritual battle primarily afflicts young men though young women are afflicted as a direct result of this. Do you agree with this? Why or why not?

4. Read Proverbs 27:17. How have you witnessed this in action? Was it successful?

5. Review the statistics in this chapter concerning the fatherless. What are your thoughts on this? Why does it seem that the faith of the father resonates more with the children than the mother or even the collective parents?

6. Have you ever witnessed the council of godly fathers described in this chapter? What are your thoughts? Was it effective?

> Defend the poor and fatherless;
> Do justice to the afflicted and needy.
>
> Psalm 82:3 (NKJV)

CHAPTER 7

SHOULD I offer you an out now?

I'll confess something. From the time I felt led to commit this work to writing, throughout the writing and editing process, all the way up through publication, I had and still have no idea how this work may be received. I've labored over this aspect.

Will it be embraced? Will it be endorsed? Will it be ignored, trivialized, demonized? You've made it this far, so I'll make a concession. I'll concede that you may not be called to open your home to the Orphan. Paul speaks of those who He gifts with singleness,

> *I want you to be without concerns. An unmarried man is concerned about the things of the Lord—how he may please the Lord.*

1 Corinthians 7:32

Singleness is a gift and those who labor in singleness actually have more time to offer the Lord. God doesn't call everyone to the altar of marriage and, similarly, He doesn't call everyone to parenthood. I honestly believe that not every person is called to be a parent. This may actually be a fleshly thought, but I know some that, personally, I would have a hard time entrusting my dog into their care, much less a child.

Nevertheless, I am praying for your consideration, that you'll see the issue for what it is and prayerfully engage the Holy Spirit on behalf of the Orphan; that the Church would embrace this for what it is.

Champions, Fathers

SCRIPTURE intensely documents God's heart for the downtrodden, the fatherless, the Orphan.

> *God in His holy dwelling is*
> *a father of the fatherless*
> *and a champion of widows.*

Psalm 68:5

> *LORD, You have heard the desire of the humble;*
> *You will strengthen their hearts.*
> *You will listen carefully,*
> *doing justice for the fatherless and the oppressed*
> *so that men of the earth may terrify them no more.*

Psalm 10:17-18

Above all, God is a father and a champion. He is a champion. He fights on behalf of His children. Indeed, He is *the* Father and He has adopted and destined many for adoption as sons with the full weight of the Promise guaranteeing eternal familial status and an invaluable inheritance found in the paternal love of the Father and the infinite walk with the Lord. The Church, at its most basic, exists as a collection of sons, a continually expanding family of which you are a member. Prayerfully, include this into your consideration.

Yet, consider that the Church has failed the Orphan. Consider that the state of Tennessee in 2013 spent roughly $630 million on the Department of Children's Services, addressing the Orphan and budgeted nearly $650 million for 2014. Consider that Tennessee DCS employs nearly 5,000 full-time workers to handle the 6,000 to 8,000 children in custody each year.[9]

Extrapolate these numbers over an entire nation and you have figures on the order of magnitude of billions of dollars and tens of thousands of workers. *Billions!* This nation spends billions of dollars on behalf of the Orphan. Consider this as you pray.

Consider that the Church has abdicated this ordained responsibility, a responsibility ordained by the entirety of the weight of God's holy Word, that the Church has abdicated this responsibility to the state.

Sitting down in my wife's nook – her semi-private study beneath the stairs – to write this last piece, it occurred to me that without adoption, I would be sitting here quite alone.

As I write, one of my foster sons furiously sweeps the garage in a desperate attempt to earn a few dollars for a mid-afternoon movie with a friend. His younger brother has taken refuge in his room, hoping he won't be included in the cleaning foray. My oldest son, Tevin, interrupts to see if I have a pair of socks for his son, my grandson – it takes me awhile to find them because Ami is in Nashville with our daughters and the little brown guys. My son Joe comes out of his room, realizes that I have ordered another to perform his job in his stead, offers a thumbs up, and then retreats to his room. My sons… I cannot fathom life without them, cannot remember life before them.

---

[9] TN FY 14 Budget Presentation, accessed March 2015, (http://state.tn.us/youth/Budget%20Presentation-2014-Final.pdf).

Our home resonates with life, with hope. In the middle of the daily scrabble of life, when the 14 year old punches the 11 year old making him cry, when the two little brown guys bicker, when the older ones stay out after curfew or get an attitude, or when they don't clean up after themselves and I find myself doing dishes for the third time that day, in the middle of all of this, it is easy to forget that this is the reality of life, of hope.

All of these things fade from meaning, from permanence, as life advances and the hope of a family's love permeates their existence. I don't know about you, but I've always had a family. I've never given a second thought to whether or not my family would be there for me. They just were, always. Even now, I take this for granted, as a given. It's not the same for them. The one foregone conclusion for them is uncertainty, uncertainty in every aspect of life to the point whereby stability and permanence seem unusual, different, unexpected, sometimes even resisted.

In Tennessee, the classes to become qualified as foster parents are called P.A.T.H. classes, Parents as Tender Healers, and I find great truth in this acronym. You see, they are wounded, grievously wounded, and most do not even realize they are wounded and like a wounded animal, many will rage against the very ones trying to assist, trying to heal. Yet, I can think of no better description of those strong enough to walk this call than Tender Healers.

Revisiting Reason

WHAT of reason and that which is unreasonable? At some point I grew weary. Several years of service with respect to the Orphan, living the Call, had produced within me a sense of fatigue that I have difficulty capturing. Ignoring the consistent blessing of the actual presence of my sons, I focused intently on the *unreasonability* of further service.

So "we" decided to take a break. As the leader of the household I declared to our family that we would take a break, we would focus upon our family for a while, we would rest some. It was exactly what we needed. Here was reason, at last. I exalted in "our" decision and intensely awaited a period of restful harmony.

Within two weeks we got the Call.

Driving home from work one particular day, my wife called and told me that she had gotten the call. DCS had taken two young boys into custody and they were sitting at the office with nowhere to go. DCS could not find a placement for them so they called Ami.

My outrage emanated forth.

No, I declared! *We talked about this! We knew this would happen! We knew that the Call would come! This was our time! This was reasonable! No! This was not our responsibility!*

Ami quietly conceded. When I arrived home a short time later, she informed me that they were still sitting at the DCS office with nowhere to go. Dinnertime came and went and still they sat, waiting. Evening came and went. Nothing. My outrage built, protecting my sense of reason. I fumed. Ami quietly informed me they were still at the office. It was nearly 9:00 p.m.

Okay, just for tonight but that's it, just an emergency placement, I defiantly agreed.

So we made the short drive downtown to the DCS office to meet these two young, blonde brothers. They sat quietly and expectantly in the surprisingly stark and barren DCS office, awaiting a fate over which they had absolutely no control.

That night, they slept on my couch as further evidence of the absolute unreasonability of this venture, a testimony to reason. Every bedroom I had was full. I had no vacancy. This was not my responsibility. Surely others must realize this and make concessions.

One day became two, then three, still no placement. Inwardly, I stewed. I raged quietly. I raged at God at that which was being asked of me. I didn't want this. These boys needed something that I just could not provide. Why must I bear this burden? Why couldn't others come alongside? Why did this have to be my responsibility?

After a couple of days, I gave it one last gasp. I summoned my daughters, aged 14 and 15 at the time, who had only recently been granted their own bedrooms after sharing a space for their entire lives to this point.

"Girls," I reasoned, "if we take these boys, you know what this means. You two will have to go back to sharing a room. You just got your own rooms and I don't know when or if you'll ever have a chance to have your own room again," I stated matter-of-factly punctuating the statement with the most earnest of looks that I could muster, willing them to submit. Unfortunately, they did just that, only not to me.

"Dad, we've already moved back in together."

"You did?" I asked, quietly, incredulously.

"Well, yeah, these boys need a place to live."

Reason faded into oblivion against that which God had ordained, proclaimed by the earnest compassion of my two faithful daughters. Today, almost two years later, these two boys stand set to become my sons. It may yet come to pass, but at a minimum, for two years they've lived as my sons and I love them as my sons, in spite of what any court may officially declare. That much I know.

My outrage builds yet again; strong is the flesh. Baby Hector's sheer existence calls me to action. When I look into his eyes, I wonder what they see in mine. Do they see the compassion steadily building or the selfish indignation? The feelings are so familiar and I know the answer. I know.

Hector needs a father. He needs a champion. God has brought me full circle yet again. If He allows it, I will be that father. I will be that champion. The circle is re-drawn once more. The tent is stretched out, ropes lengthened. I'll drive these tent pegs deeper still, burying them in the Word of the Lord our God that they may never break loose. I cannot do less. I cannot resist the Call one second longer. It is the will of God. Of this much I am certain.

A Final Call

YET, maybe this is not your call, I'll concede yet again. Maybe God has called you to something different. Perhaps God has called you to a different walk, but perhaps they are not mutually exclusive. Perhaps He has called you to that, whatever it may be, *and* to this call, the call of the Orphan. Perhaps God has called you to more than one thing.

As you prayerfully consider what has been laid before you, consider speaking with someone about it. Find a foster or adoptive family and speak to them. Ask them the hard questions. Make them tell you the good, the bad, the ugly. Familiarize yourself with the issue. Read, study. Search God's Word. Examine your locality. Most of all, search your heart. Examine your own heart.

Decide to get involved and God will lead you; He will direct you. Maybe God is calling you to provide resources – money, time, food, clothing – to those persons and organizations that care for the Orphan. Maybe God is calling you to reach out to a family that has opened their own home and offer them support, prayer, encouragement. Maybe God has called you to become a member and get involved in a local organization that addresses the Orphan, to advocate on behalf of the Orphan.

Maybe God is calling you to actually open your home. Consider all of these things. In prayer, consider the Call, the call that this work has examined, the call of God that speaks loud and clear from the pages of Scripture, versus the of-spoken of but seldom discerned or followed mysterious and furtive whisperings from an unbiblical deity.

All of this to say that God has called each of us to the remarkable, not the ordinary, not the reasonable, not the certain. In ministering to those most afflicted, the least of these, the Orphan, God has continuously shown me that…

there is *No Higher Call.*

> The LORD watches over the strangers;
> He relieves the fatherless and widow;
> But the way of the wicked
> He turns upside down.
>
> Psalm 146:9 (NKJV)

Bradford Smith

Final Discussion Questions

QUESTIONS

1. Read Psalm 68:1-6.

    a. What is the significance of God being referred to as a father to the fatherless and a champion of widows.

    b. What does God "do" in verse 6?

    c. How is this significant in Jewish history re: the remainder of the Psalm?

    d. How does this translate to the Church?

2. Considering what you have read, what would you say is God's overall stance on physical adoption?

3. Considering what you have read, grade the Church's response to the overall issue of the Orphan.

4. How does your local church respond to the issue?

5. How have you responded?

6. How has the Holy Spirit spoken to you during this study? Do you agree/disagree with the overall premise of this work? Why or why not?

> The LORD watches over the strangers;
> He relieves the fatherless and widow;
> But the way of the wicked
> He turns upside down.
>
> Psalm 146:9 (NKJV)

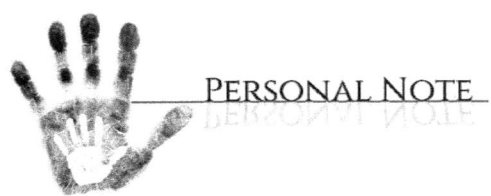

PERSONAL NOTE

THANK you so very much for taking the time to read *No Higher Call*. I pray that you'll consider getting involved.

Do you know that orphans, children with no family, live in your city, available for immediate adoption? Do you know that your local Department of Children's Services is desperate for foster families?

There is a tiny hand out there desperately reaching to take your hand, to feel safe and secure and loved possibly for the first time.

You can make an eternal difference in a child's life. I cannot think of many things more important than that.

In Christ,

Brad

BIBLIOGRAPHY

Bonhoeffer, Dietrich.
The Cost of Discipleship.
Touchstone: New York, 1959.

Platt, David.
Radical.
Multnomah Books: Colorado Springs, 2010.

GLOSSARY

Eschatology – the study of the teachings in the Bible concerning the end times or of the period of time dealing with the return of Christ and the events that follow.

Hermeneutics – the science of interpretation. Theologically, and biblically, speaking it is the means by which a person examines the Bible to determine what it means.

Immutability – Unchangeable. Permanent. The divine attribute of unchangeableness. God said in Exodus 3:14, "I AM that I AM"; signifying his eternal sameness and his sovereignty. He cannot change his moral character, his love, his omniscience, omnipresence, omnipotence, etc. God is "From everlasting to everlasting," (Psalm 90:2).

Impassibility – part of God's immutability (changelessness) such that he is not affected by what happens in the world. It means that God is not subject to passions such as pain and suffering, i.e., those things which act upon him and with which he has no control. God is not acted upon, but he acts upon us.

Parousia – A Greek term meaning arrival or coming. The term is often referred to as the time of Christ's return, hence, the *Parousia*, i.e., 2 Thessalonians 2:1

Pneuma– breath (Greek

Ruach – spirit (Hebrew)

Protoevangelium —The term for the first declaration of the gospel, which occurs in Genesis 3:15. It is a prophecy that Christ will overcome the devil and redeem mankind. The first proclamation of the Gospel comes immediately after the fall of Adam and Eve and shows God's intention of saving men from sin.

Regeneration – The act of God whereby he renews the spiritual condition of a sinner. It is a spiritual change brought about by the work of the Holy Spirit so that the person then possesses new life–eternal life. Regeneration is a change in our moral and spiritual nature where justification is a change in our relationship with God.

Transcendence – a theological term that, when referring to the Christian God, states that God is outside of the universe and is independent of it and its properties. God is "other," "different" from his creation. He is independent and different from his creatures (Isaiah 55:8-9). He transcends his creation. He is beyond it and not limited by it or to it.

THE AUTHOR

BRADFORD SMITH has been married to his best friend Ami since 2001 and they stay busy raising their nine children together. A graduate of West Point, Brad has served on active duty since 1995 including multiple combat tours to Iraq and Afghanistan.

In 2007, Brad surrendered to the call to preach and in 2011 he joined the staff of The Way, A Baptist Church in Clarksville, as the Missions Pastor where he continues to serve bi-vocationally.

In 2010, Brad and Ami opened the Clarksville Covenant House for teenagers who age out of the foster system and in 2013, Brad graduated from Liberty Theological Seminary with a Masters of Divinity.

Once the Army releases him from duty, he plans to plant a new Baptist church and run the Covenant House full time alongside his wife.

www.thewayofclarksville.com

www.thewayofclarksville.com/covenant-house

ALSO AVAILABLE

SCOURGE

"Confronting the Global Issue of Addiction"

By Bradford Smith

CHEMICAL addiction wreaks havoc across a broadening swath of society leading those who suffer toward certain destruction. Never before has humanity been so afflicted.

Scourge takes a heart-wrenching, unexpected first-hand look at the spiritual aspect of this deadly assault upon the very souls of mankind. Of those who struggle, some find devastation and death while others find redemption and life.

> "Brad Smith leads us on a journey through the lives of the scourged. He does so much more than chronicle the struggle. He draws you into their life where you will experience the frustration and hopelessness of the battle and the joy of victory found in Christ Jesus."
>
> – Paul Scott, Community Impact Pastor, Hilldale Baptist Church

Available now wherever fine books are sold.

MORE TO COME

BRAVE RIFLES

"The Theology of Warfare"

By Bradford Smith

FOR millenia, man has waged war. Clausewitz, Sun Tzu, Jomini: all sought to understand the nature of conflict itself. ***Brave Rifles*** goes further, examining the true heart of warfare.

What does the Bible say concerning warfare? How should a Christian conduct himself while engaged in warfare? What does God think about warfare?

This is a long overdue work, desperately needed by the modern warrior.

Coming soon from Bradford Smith and Olivia Kimbrell Press™.

www.ingramcontent.com/pod-product-compliance
Lightning Source LLC
LaVergne TN
LVHW020933090426
835512LV00020B/3337